As I Am Presently Known

To the talented and ever-lovely Tia! ♥ Emily

Leon Rubinstein
with Emily Rubin

Plain View Press
P. O. 42255
Austin, TX 78704

plainviewpress.net
sb@plainviewpress.net
512-441-2452

ISBN: 978-0-911051-03-2
Library of Congress Number: 2009929324

Cover by Robert Levers.

Acknowledgments

To my son, Wade Rubinstein, without whom this book would not be possible. I would like to thank him for the time that he took away from his loving and devoted wife, Jill Block, and his children, Max and Ellie.

To Estelle, my loving wife, my one and only, whose support and love has sustained me.

To my beautiful daughter, Debra Peak, who always encouraged me and stood by me. To her dear husband, Gary Peak, and my three granddaughters, Laurel, Robyn and Sydney.

Many thanks to Emily Rubin, who put the story together with her expertise, advice, patience, and kindness.

Contents

Foreword

The story of the Jewish people in the twentieth century is one of the great dramas of modern times. It has everything, from the searing tragedy of the Holocaust to the heroic creation of the State of Israel to the emergence of the Jewish community in the United States as the largest and most successful Jewish community in the world. Most people, when they search for the human dimension to these epochal events, come to know the Holocaust through the writings of Anne Frank or Elie Wiesel. They see Israel through the eyes of David Ben-Gurion or Golda Meir. When I look for the human story of what it must have felt like to be a Jew in the twentieth century, I think of my friend and congregant Leon Rubinstein.

Leon experienced it all. Born into the comfortable security of a loving family in a small town in Poland, he would see his world fall apart when the Nazis invaded. He saw his parents led away to be murdered, he experienced the kindness of a Polish Christian and the cruelty of other Polish Christians. After the war, he made his way to Israel, served in the Israeli army and then found a new life and family in America.

I am glad that Leon has chosen to write his memories down in this book, because I know how much those memories mean to him and how important it is for his children and grandchildren to know what kind of world we live in and what sort of experiences shaped him into the person he is. But I hope that many other people will read them as well, because Leon's story is the story of many people, not all of whom were as strong-willed or as fortunate as he was, and the memory of what happened to them is too precious to be lost.

May Leon enjoy his years of retirement surrounded by people who love him, and may his memoir be a lasting tribute to a world that no longer exists and to the life that was his.

Harold Kushner
Rabbi Laureate of Temple Israel of Natick

This is the story of a wealthy man. Leon Rubinstein's wealth is not to be measured in dollars, but more so in the values of confidence, faith, zest for life, and love of family. In the Jewish wisdom literature, Pirkei Avot, we learn "Think about three things, and you will avoid sin: Know from where you've come, know your destination, and know before Whom you stand." (Avot 3:1) Leon treasures the heritage of a loving family steeped in Jewish tradition. Truly, he has not always known his destination. But he always faced the next turn of fate with hope, openness, and humanity. Through ravages of war and persecution, survival, and in times of good fortune, Leon has held the same faith, that the teachings of Jewish life and a belief in God were firm foundations on which to build a life. That life, described here in his own words, draws the reader close to Leon. When I hear Leon's story, I feel deep gratitude for the beautiful friendship that we've shared for many years.

Robert S. Scherr
Jewish Chaplain, Williams College
Hazzan Emeritus, Temple Israel of Natick

Preface

In the spring of 2007, I traveled to Israel on business. My first stop there was Haifa, a port city in the north. My hotel was situated on a ridge high up on Mount Carmel. Across the hotel lobby was a white marble patio, which offered panoramic views of Haifa harbor and the Carmel mountain range. Standing on the patio, watching ships pass in and out of the harbor, I recalled the story of my father's arrival in this same port in the spring of 1946.

My father, Leon Rubinstein, arrived in Haifa as part of the Ha'apala, the "illegal" immigration of Jewish refugees from Europe to Palestine. Traveling with a group of children orphaned by the Holocaust, he came to Palestine in search of a new beginning. He had nowhere else to go.

I envisioned my father as a boy of sixteen, standing on the crowded deck of a steamer, staring wide-eyed at the horizon. The city of Haifa and the headlands of Mount Carmel must have been a welcoming sight. Finally, after months of anticipation, he had arrived in Eretz Yisrael. The Land of Israel.

As I recalled my father's story, I felt tears streaming down my cheeks. I was overwhelmed by his journey from Poland to Palestine. I felt grateful for my father's survival. I felt grateful for the gift of his stories.

My father seldom talked about his childhood and his years in Israel. From the bits and pieces gathered over my lifetime, I knew the outline of my father's early life. Missing were the details. Finally, in 2002, at the age of 72, my father agreed to tell his story. Sitting down with him at his kitchen table in Falmouth, Massachusetts, I listened. After all those years, I was amazed by how vibrant his memories were. The details filled in the outline and connected me to my father's past. This memoir is the result of those kitchen table conversations.

Through his story, I share my father's losses. I also share in the memories that sustain him. Foremost, I share his hope that telling his story will help heal the world.

Wade Rubinstein
April 2008

Note to Readers

When I first met Leon, I was struck by his voice. It was the voice of experience and wisdom, compassion and humor, insightful even when speaking of suffering and deep pain. It was also tremendously rich and particular, yielding the echoes of many languages, captivating idioms and turns of phrase. It was this vibrant, expressive individual that I wanted to capture in *As I Am Presently Known*. To that end, the Rubinsteins and I agreed that Leon's memoir would be written in a conversational tone, so that readers would be able to experience his unique voice.

The book chronicles the events that shaped Leon's life from his birth in 1930 to 1954, his 24th year. The book begins with Leon's happy, formative years with his close-knit Jewish family in Eastern Poland. It then traces his path through the devastating war years, to British Palestine, the founding of the State of Israel, and his ultimate journey to the United States, where he meets his beautiful wife, Estelle, and settles into Jewish American life. Having achieved a new beginning, Leon concludes his memoir in 1954.

Throughout my rendering of Leon's story, I deliberately avoid editorialization. Soon after the setting is established, individuals and events are brought to life through action, detail, and dialogue. Leon recounts his experiences – sometimes disturbing and haunting, often heroic and life-affirming – in an unflinching, straightforward manner. This "show, not tell" mode of storytelling naturally draws the reader into a search for meaning: How does Leon overcome such catastrophic personal loss? Is it possible to forgive the perpetrators of the Holocaust? As a survivor, can one make peace with the past?

To address these questions, and to provide a more comprehensive and reflective portrayal of Leon, an extended conversation with him appears in the final part of the book. In "Looking Back: A Conversation with Leon Rubinstein," Leon talks openly about how he manages the traumas he endured as a child and a young man, and how he views the world around him. He speaks explicitly and sensitively of war, fatherhood, and the role of Judaism in his life.

A word on sources. The interviews Wade Rubinstein recorded of his father in 2002 were of great assistance to me. Using these invaluable recordings as a foundation for the book, as well as conducting additional interviews with Leon in person and over the phone, I was able to assemble the fascinating and complex story of Leon's life. A fair amount of historical research was also involved. I consulted texts on the Holocaust and the history of the Jewish people, archival video footage of Poland in the 1930s and 1940s, Yiddish language dictionaries, retired atlases and online publications.

It has been an honor to work with the Rubinstein family while writing this book. I would like to thank Wade and Leon for their patient cooperation with numerous requests, such as constructing a timeline of events, confirming key locations, dates and names, and collaboratively reviewing several drafts of the manuscript throughout the writing process. I would also like to thank my own family for their support and encouragement. Thank you especially to Rose and Lew Rubin, Matt Grant, and N.S. Koenings, for your keen editorial eyes.

Emily Rubin
M.A. English/Writing
emily_rubin@hotmail.com
(978) 318-9665

I. Childhood in Poland, 1930-1945

Map of Central Europe, 1938.
© Rand McNally. Reproduced with permission R.L.08-S–63

My Family Home

My name is Leon Rubinstein, as I am presently known. I was born to a Jewish family in 1930 in the town of Koretz, Poland. Before the Holocaust, there were such happy times in my family. I had one brother, Froyem, and five sisters, Ana, Anyeh, Chayele, Luba and Batya. My parents were Wolf and Edith. For the first six years of my life, we rented a single story dwelling that measured twenty feet by twenty feet. Our home was adjacent to a beautiful grassy field, always green in the summer. That's where we had our open-air market each week. In warm weather, traveling performers entertained us there. Most of them were gypsies that drifted from one town to another. They set up tents in the field and assembled a wooden merry-go-round. A trotting horse pulled it or the gypsies pushed it with their strong arms.

Our house had a thatched straw roof. The floor was covered with a chalky, reddish paint that made it hard and durable. We swept on a daily basis to keep the floor clean. Our furniture was primitive, just wooden boxes on the dirt floor. For beds, we filled the wooden boxes with straw, covered the straw with a sheet and blankets, and that was where we slept. Pillows were made from goose feathers. Expensive mattresses were made from goose feathers, too. But they had to be treated carefully and people like us couldn't afford them.

Our rooms were small. My mother and father slept in one bedroom with the youngest children. A few other children slept in another small room. The rest of us slept in the common room near the hot stove, two or three children to a bed. During the day, the bed in the common room was covered with a blanket for a sitting area. Our house was decorated simply. Just a black and white photograph of relatives on the wall. We had small windows, poorly insulated. A cast iron stove for burning wood. Most of the homes in Koretz had brick ovens, heated by wood, to bake challahs and breads and pastries. But the house we rented didn't have an oven. So we did all the cooking on the stove. My father manipulated the fire in such a way that he could actually bake on the stove, too.

In back, we had an outhouse. It was three and a half feet by three and a half feet wide. Just a closet with a hole in the ground. When the hole got filled, we took a shovel and dug another hole to bury the waste.

My grandparents, uncles, aunts and cousins were all within walking distance. And our synagogue was near the open field by our home. We called it *shul*. Every Saturday, every holiday, we went to shul because we were observant Jews.

Sometimes, before a big holiday like Passover, we bought new clothes in a store, though we didn't get more than one item. We bought socks or a shirt or a pair of shoes that lasted until who knows how long. Then they were passed on to my brother and sisters. My mother sewed most of our clothes at home. We had a few round buttons made of wood, and she used them over and over.

The Korchyk River ran in a U-shape around the town. Every day we walked nearly a mile to the river to get water. Quite a bit of exercise we had. No wonder I was so skinny. In winter and summer, all of the children *schlepped* water. Even children as young as five or six years old went down to the river with a couple of pails and a stick on their shoulders that's called a yoke. We dropped one pail in the river and pulled it out by a rope. Dropped in the other pail and filled that up, too. We carried our water by hooking up the pails to the yoke. It was the first thing we did after school.

In winter, sometimes the water hole was frozen over because it hadn't been used in the last hour or two. Then we'd have to break the ice. No matter what, we never came back without water. We had a wooden water barrel at the side of our house and that barrel had to be filled every day. We relied on that water for all of our needs. Washing, cooking, drinking. I wouldn't drink from the Korchyk River today, but in those days the water was clear and tasty.

Aside from getting water, us children had many chores. Chopping wood, straightening the house, looking after my younger sisters. Sometimes when I finished my chores, I'd look for a friend to play with. But if the other boy hadn't finished his chores, he couldn't go out. That happened a lot. So I picked myself up and went back home. My sisters and brother were always around.

In 1936, my father bought a bigger house at 25 Manasterskya Street, not far from our first home in Koretz. The owners of the new house had moved to a different town thirty-five miles away. My father bicycled all the way to the other town to purchase the house. One of my father's businesses was bicycle assembly, so we were lucky we always had one or two bikes at home.

Koretz was the type of small town where people really knew each other, so we knew who our neighbors were going to be. Our new street was lined with several large churches, and there was a police station on the corner, but our immediate neighbors were Jewish. There was a dentist and a couple of widows on our street. In the house across from us was a wealthy man with two daughters. He traded in animal skins and shoe leather. I could smell his deliveries because there was still flesh on the skins. The goods were left in a woven basket on his porch. Probably he stored them in his common room. Mind you, these homes did not have basements. In the summer, we used a root celler, hole in the corner of the kitchen to keep the vegetables cool. It was below floor level, around 50 degrees Fahrenheit. We kept it covered with a piece of wood and lined with stones to stay cold. When we needed to store a piece of meat overnight, we put it in the hole. Most of the time, though, we cooked it right away.

When we first came into our new house, it was empty. And so spacious. Finally, something we had of our own. That house was one floor with two bedrooms, and a huge common area where we cooked and worked and played. There was a good-sized porch that protruded five feet in front of the house. A little outhouse in back. And we had a brick oven lined with broken glass in the bottom to absorb the heat. The oven needed repairs and right away my father found someone to fix it. There was a round opening in the front where my father baked bread, and the wood burned in the back. Soon, the warm, sweet smell of baking filled the house.

My brother Froyem and me and a couple sisters slept in the corner bedroom with one window. My mother and father had the bedroom next to ours, and like our first house, they always had a few children in there. Whoever else needed a bed, they slept in the common room.

The new house also had dirt floors. The walls of the house were wood and the roof was made of red brick tiles that interlocked. During hailstorms, the gale picked up the tiles and slammed them against the roof. Sounded like "Bang! Bang! Bang!" There was no insulation. In winter, the wood stove was going all the time to keep the house warm. The men that delivered firewood stacked it by the side of the house.

We had big, heavy snowstorms. Once we couldn't get out the door. We went into the attic, picked up some tiles and climbed right out the roof. Keep in mind, we didn't have snow shovels back then. We used a regular dirt shovel to make a path to the door. And nobody plowed streets in those days. We worked our way through the snow, tried to pack it down with the shovel. We wore a lot of layers in the wintertime. Went to bed with even more. This was the way to stay warm. The temperature dropped to freezing cold in that part of the world.

Electricity was available a year and a half after we moved to Manasterskya Street, but we couldn't afford to put it in until the latter part of 1938. That's when my father put in two light bulbs. One in the cooking area, one in the common area. The cable was visible, just two strands of wire going from one bulb to the other. The wires were twisted together and passed along the ceiling. At the end of each month, we got a note about usage. And then we paid.

Our record player we listened to constantly. We had maybe two dozen shellac records, some classical, some Yiddish. This was before vinyl records were produced. The sound was scratchy because the records were so heavily used. The record player broke down a lot, but my father found ways to fix it. One time, the record player broke and my father decided to make a gear out of bone. The new gear had to match the old one, which was made of brass. First, he took a large piece of bone that he found. It must have come from a cow or some other animal and didn't quite work because it was too brittle. So he decided to use an animal horn.

He probably got the idea during *Rosh Hashanah*, when he was at shul and saw the *shofar*, the ram's horn, and realized it would make a good gear. Off he went to the kosher slaughterhouse in town and got a piece of horn. He worked on the gear at night, since he couldn't waste time during the workday. With a file and a knife, he did some cutting and some scraping, and he made the gear. It lasted for years. We used to sit and talk about it. I learned a lot from that, like you can't mix gears from different metals together. You need to have something in between, like a piece of plastic. But plastic wasn't available, so he used the horn.

The books we had in the house were mostly *siddurim*. Prayer books. There were a few music books and books associated with schooling that were left over from the year before. Books for the first, second, third grade, and math books were there. We also had books for learning Hebrew. But no leisurely books. It was nothing like the type of books people have at home now.

At the side of our house, we had a sunny piece of land with a few trees. Some of the trees bore fruit. Apples and pears. The nicest trees were on my neighbor's property. They had cherry trees. I snuck under their fence in the mornings. Whatever fell down from their trees, I picked up and brought home. That fruit was so fresh and tangy.

On our land, I started a garden each summer from seeds. I grew my first garden when I was seven and I had one each year until 1939 when the war broke out. I grew carrots, lettuce, scallions, cucumbers, all sorts of vegetables. Big, meaty tomatoes. Spicy, round radishes. The growing season was short but the garden grew fast since the soil was rich. Never used any fertilizer and not much water either, because I had to schlep the water from the river. After a few days of dry weather, the rain would come and give the garden a good soaking.

When the weather grew cold, some vegetables were left because we didn't harvest it all. Mostly radishes and root vegetables left in the ground. Well, those vegetables attracted rodents. I used to walk on the morning of a first snow and find animal footprints in the garden. I'd try to evaluate the footprints. Was it a rat or a more exotic animal that came to my garden? One day, I saw a really unusual footprint. Brought my father outside to show him. He said to me, "Lazer, this has got to be a mink because of the spread of the legs." After all, minks have stretched-out bodies. He thought the skin might be worth something. Told me not to touch the footprint. Later that day, he brought over a guy who trapped animals for a living. The hunter set a trap and caught the animal. But it wasn't the mink my father hoped for. It was just a common animal. Maybe a fox.

When I close my eyes, I can see Manasterskya Street like I was there yesterday. It was a big step up from our first home, a real improvement. Much more living space. The house was thirty feet long and twenty feet wide. We even rode a bicycle back and forth the length of the house in winter. In summer, we sat on the porch in a rocking bench my father built. It held six people. When we finished our chores, we sat there and rocked. And watched the day slip by.

Leon's mother, Edith Rubinstein,
Koretz, Poland, date unknown.

Meals and Holidays

My father did most of the baking in our house. My mother baked small things, maybe a cake now and then. But my father baked half a dozen breads every Thursday, and it was something special. He took time off from work and baked enough bread for the week. Most were dark breads. He baked four or five *challahs* and pastries for the Sabbath. Those breads always tasted rich and fresh. Never grew stale. Many times, my father bought grain and we ground our own flour. We'd watch him sift the flour, mix the ingredients, braid the challah. He always bragged about his oven. The best oven in Koretz. Sometimes he filled a duck with all sorts of stuffing

Leon's father, Wolf Rubinstein.
Koretz, Poland, date unknown.

and put it in the oven to cook slowly. When it was done, the meat fell right off the bones.

While my father did the baking, my mother and sisters made the meals. In those days, cooking was a real chore. A lot of work to prepare a meal. Nobody cooked every day. We cooked two or three times a week and stored the leftovers in the hole in the ground. For everyday meals, we had two sets of plates to keep kosher. One set for meat and one for dairy. Breakfast was a hard-boiled egg, plenty of bread with butter, and maybe some cottage cheese. Lunch was often a piece of bread with some chicken fat instead of butter. That was the *schmaltz*. We took fat from the chicken and kept it in the ground so it stayed in a chilly state. We also put on *grivens*, which was made from the skin of the chicken. The women sauteed the loose chicken skin in a frying pan with some onions until it curled up and became crispy. So we put the schmaltz on the bread with a couple of grivens and then a slice of onion, because that provided the flavor. We used to make our own jams, so occasionally lunch was a slice of bread with butter and plum jam. With meals we drank a cup of tea, sometimes cocoa. Everybody in the family liked sugar, and it was easy to get because there was a sugar factory in town. Hard to get salt, but sugar was available.

For dinner sometimes we had a cutlet, which was beef with lots of garlic and onions. We didn't have a grinder so the women would take a cheap cut of meat and chop at it with a cleaver on a wooden board. It was tough meat so a lot of chopping went into it. They mixed that with garlic, onions, some grivens and the schmaltz. They added an egg, then shaped the mixture into patties and fried that on top of the wood stove. Cutlets we had with plenty of bread. Occasionally, my mother took a piece of meat and a lot of potatoes and baked that in the brick oven, almost like a brisket. My mother made some flavorful meals, no doubt about it. Times were good then. We were never hungry. We had plenty of food until the war broke out. But we didn't have extra plates. When guests came over, two or three kids would share one plate. And utensils were not there, so we used our fingers. For soup, we had to wait for a spoon.

At every meal, my father sat at the head of the table. He was not a tall man. Five feet, five inches. But a strong, well built guy with dark eyes and dark hair. We knew who was in charge. If one of the children was showing off at dinner, my father just looked at him. Then the child would settle down. One look was all we needed.

My father was *Shomer Shabbos* and came home early on Fridays. He was self-employed so he could do that. Shabbos was a big, big day for us. On Friday mornings, my mother went to her special butcher and bought one chicken. And out of that chicken, she and my sisters would prepare a tremendous meal. She started with soup made from the flavor of chicken. The women added bones from the chicken legs or the wings, or the neck that we called a *gorgle*. They made *knaidlach*, Jewish dumplings, and put that in the chicken soup. The main course was a small piece of meat. She was capable of generating all these things from one chicken. Fed a family of nine. Of course, we had freshly baked challah. Sometimes we had *gefilte fish*, which was mostly starch with the smell of fish. The women had this knack of taking a little bit of fish and adding breadcrumbs and potatoes. A beautiful dish of gefilte fish.

Shabbos was an occasion. An event we looked forward to the whole week. My father made sure everyone was washed up and dressed in clean clothes. At sunset, we sat together at a large table in the eating area. My mother would gather my sisters to light the candles and chant the blessing. It was called *bensching*. She wouldn't start bensching the candles until all the girls were together, from little to the oldest one. After we got electricity, I wondered, "Why do we have to go through with the candle lighting?" After all, we had light bulbs. But my family maintained the tradition. That's the way it was done. My father would make blessings, a *kiddush* over the wine and a *motzi* over the challah. We sat and ate and sang songs. Sucked on chicken bones inside and out. People don't clean up a bone the way we used to. Those Friday night meals lasted forever.

Because we were observant, we never lit a fire on Saturday. The oven was used on Friday and we put a lid on it so it stayed warm. The next day, the women heated up food in the oven or on the cast iron stove. When we returned from Saturday shul, my mother served *cholent*, a hearty stew made of beans and barley. After these meals, my father took a nap. He went to the side of the house where we had fruit trees. He'd climb to the top of an apple tree and disappear. He'd find a branch and make himself comfortable. And in this way, he drifted to sleep. A couple times he fell off the tree. But he didn't fall far and he landed on soft, pillowy soil.

My family celebrated every Jewish holiday. *Shabbos, Purim, Passover, Rosh Hashanah, Yom Kippur, Sukkot, Simchas Torah.* The big shuls had large choirs and some of them imported choirs from other towns, so it was very festive. Our shul was a thirty by forty foot building with a wooden floor and accommodated about a hundred-twenty people. The men sat in a circle and the *bimah*, the raised platform, was in the center. Preparing shul for the holidays was a communal event for us boys who hadn't had our bar mitzvahs. We painted and cleaned and polished the woodwork with oil until it shined. When the holiday arrived, all of us were together in this ritually pure building. When I walked past the men wrapped in their cloth *tallises*, I could smell what they ate for dinner, because the tallises held the scent of their food.

The services were lengthy. The rabbis didn't skip a thing and they didn't rush it, either. They started the service early in the morning and stretched it out until two, three o'clock in the afternoon for the High Holidays. During Yom Kippur, we stayed even later because we were fasting. My father left the house early and didn't come back until the service was over. My mother and sisters would rush home to start setting the table and preparing to break the fast. When we finally sat down, we sang the blessings over the meal before we ate. We talked about the holiday and what it meant. Each bite of food tasted better than the last.

After a long winter, we looked forward to Passover. It was the beginning of spring, and spring we associated with the outdoors. Weeks before the holiday started, we began planning and preparing. The way I knew Passover was coming was my father would start shopping for good quality geese. He bought them from Christians who raised them to be sold because Jews didn't do that. A goose was a bird different in taste than a chicken. With such a large family, my father tried to get two or three. The largest birds he could find. We kept them in the house and fed them grain. Tried to fatten them up. Watch that bird gain another pound or two. Me, my sisters, my brother, my parents, we all fed them. Those birds ate almost twenty-four hours. It was like having a pet in the house but it was also a game to see who could get them the fattest.

After a few weeks, my father would take the geese to get slaughtered by a *shochet*, a kosher butcher. Nobody else went, even though we wanted to see how it was done. After the geese were killed, my father had a special way of fattening them even more. He'd blow them up with air and put a plug in them so the air couldn't escape. They'd stay in that shape without collapsing and the meat would be tenderized. Our chore was taking the feathers off the birds so my mother could make a fresh feather pillow. We made sure none of those feathers flew around the house. Then we got the house ready for Passover. We carried the Passover plates down from the attic and moved the regular dishes out of the way. Since the Passover plates had to be made clean for the holiday, we scrubbed them thoroughly. And each pail of water for scrubbing dishes we hauled from the river.

At Passover, no Jewish family ate leavened bread. Only *matzo*. So we had to get rid of the *chometz*, the traces of leavened bread. My father went through a ceremony to ritually clean the house of chometz, by burning bread crusts and bread crumbs. Some of our cousins would paint their house to get rid of the chometz. In those days, painting the house meant painting everything. The walls and the floors.

There was a Jewish bakery nearby that only baked matzos. The entire production was supervised by the rabbis so the process took a while. The rabbis made sure the flour mill, even though it was owned by Jews, was properly cleaned for grinding the flour. Sometimes us kids would go to the bakery early in the morning to see if we could get a little piece of matzo. Maybe a piece that was cracked or didn't stay in shape. We didn't dare step into the kitchen, where the men baked the matzos in a production line. Every once in a while, one of the bakers called over to the young man who delivered matzos. Told him to do a delivery. Mind you, the bakery didn't get orders by phone. People stopped by, put a note up for matzos and paid for them. Usually they couldn't buy their whole order at once. They'd buy enough for a few days and then come back to buy more. We got deliveries for the first few days and then the last few days of Passover. The matzos were round, about eight or ten inches in diameter. Delivered in a woven basket.

The children's job at Passover was grinding matzo meal with a huge mortar and pestle. We called it "a hunk of wood," and it was as high as a table. Had to bend our knees and support it between our legs. We took matzos and broke them up as much as we could with our hands. Then we dropped the pieces in the mortar and banged it with what looked like a big baseball bat. We had to make enough matzo meal to last the entire week of Passover. My mother used the matzo meal to bake cakes and make knaidlach for soup. I don't think any Jewish family went out and bought matzo meal ready-made. Each family made it themselves.

There were days and days of cooking. All of us participated. When the Passover *seder* came, we knew every detail that had gone into the preparations. We set the table with matzos, the shank bone, the boiled egg. And we put out *maror*, the bitter herb, and *haroset*, the honey-sweetened, chopped fruit. Salt water for dipping *karpas*, the green vegetable. The cup of wine for the prophet Elijah. My dad read the *Haggadah*, the story of the exodus from Egypt, from beginning to end. The youngest child asked the four questions about the purpose of the holiday. We told stories and sang all the Passover songs. The seder lasted until the wee hours of the morning.

The one holiday I don't remember celebrating in my family was birthdays. If it was done, it was probably combined with a Shabbos meal. Though there wasn't a focus on birthdays, we always celebrated when a baby arrived. We brought a rabbi into the house and he did the naming for each of my sisters. When a boy child was born to a family, his *bris* was an event in the community. It was mainly an affair for children. Cookies were baked, friends were invited.

Batya, my youngest sister, was the only one who wasn't born at home. She was the born in the hospital because the Russians were in control by then. It was 1939 and there was free medicine. My mother was encouraged to go to the hospital and she stayed overnight. We came to visit her. She got a small piece of cake with her meal. Something so good she wanted to share with us. Each one got a tiny taste. Just a smell of that cake. She never baked anything like it because not all those ingredients were available.

Many foods were hard to get. We had no citrus fruit in the house because that was a specialty. The first time we ever saw an orange, we watched my mother peel it. Very gently she separated the slices. Gave one to each of us. The flavor exploded in my mouth. It tasted so good I wanted to eat the skin on the orange. But that was saved for later, to be used in the cooking or baking. Nothing was ever wasted.

Leon's mother, Edith Rubinstein; maternal grandmother, Lea Weiner; and father, Wolf Rubinstein, Koretz, Poland, date unknown.

My Parents and Grandparents

My father, Wolf, was born in 1904. His family was from Zhytomyr, Russia, a town ninety miles east of Koretz. My paternal grandfather died when my father was a child. And I was named for him. Lazer Rubinstein. In 1918, my father was brought to Koretz by his mother. During that time, there were pogroms. For no reason, gentiles would launch attacks on Jewish villages, tyrannizing the Jews. I presume my grandmother moved her family over for safety reasons, and she had acquaintances in Koretz. My father was a good son. He was smart, he was resourceful. He came to Koretz and settled in quite well. A few years later, he married my mother.

After my grandfather died, my father's mother married a gentleman who took her to America around 1936 or 1937. Someplace in the Detroit area. I was never able to locate her there, though I tried for many years. My grandmother's name was Batya, and my youngest sister was named after her. My father spoke fondly of his mother, that she was a kind, loving person. I saw photographs of her. A short, round-faced little lady with straight hair. She corresponded with my father on an annual basis. Maybe once a year before the holidays, a letter came. My father had several married sisters. One sister in Zhytomyr and two others, Esther and Batsia, who emigrated to Argentina in the 1920s.

Edith, my mother, was also born in 1904. She grew up in Koretz. My mother's father, Avram, was a well-established trader in horses. He would buy horses from one guy and sell them to another guy. Most of the trades happened in the open-air market near our old house. Every Thursday, farmers came to town and brought their goods. Mostly they had vegetables. Sometimes flowers, sometimes oil or seeds for oil. My grandfather was always there with two or three horses and sometimes he even had cattle to sell to the butchers. Believe me, cattle wasn't something you put in a tractor and drove to town. He acquired the cattle by going to a farm and buying the animals. Then he walked the cattle to town, sometimes for miles.

Avram made a good living. With his wife Lea he had a large family, eight children. Six sons and two daughters. They were all industrious. Two of the sons, Menashe and Yosef, were glaziers. They installed glass windows. One son was a barber. Another was a horse trader. One son passed away from an illness when he was a young man. The younger daughter, my aunt, had a shop in Koretz where she sold her own ice cream. It was a small business, popular during the summer. She was not married, though she had a suitor. Like most of the family, she was killed in the Holocaust when she was twenty-eight or thirty years old. One son, the lucky one, left for the United States before the war. That was Harry.

My mother Edith was lovely to look at, with long, shiny, black hair. She wasn't that strong, but she was healthy. All of my sisters had long hair, too, because my mother loved long hair. The girls cared for each other's hair and washed it with kerosene to keep it clean. There was always that strong odor around them. It was the same kerosene we used in lamps to provide light at night, before we had electricity. Since the men and boys had short hair, we just washed it with soap. But for long hair, the kerosene kept lice at bay.

I haven't the slightest idea how my parents met, but I have a feeling it was prearranged. At that time, people tried to make arrangements for marriages. Men and women didn't have much chance to intermingle. I have a feeling my father and Edith's father met at shul. Somebody might have recommended my father to Avram. Maybe they said, "Wolf's a man from Zhytomyr. His father passed away. He's got a mother here. He's hardworking. He already set himself up in business."

My mother thought the world of my father. There was nothing he couldn't do. She always bragged about him. "Your daddy's a genius." Our house was crowded, so they couldn't hide their affection for one another. There was a lot of hugging that went on between them. It was nothing unusual to drop in on them in their bedroom. No locks on the door. At shul they sat apart, but they walked from shul together. He carried his tallis bag and she held his hand. Once or twice a year, my father took my mother to the Jewish theater in town.

And, of course, my mother was very warm to her own family. Before her father passed away in his house, she was there constantly. He caught pneumonia at fifty-five years old. It began with a cold and he never stopped coughing. A week and a half later, my grandfather was gone. He died in the morning and the funeral was held that afternoon. There was no such thing as bringing the body to a morgue or a funeral parlor. The people that handled this came to the house and took over. They washed the body and wrapped it in a tallis or sheet. There was no casket in those days. The body was put in a grave and covered with dirt, with not even a board on top. My grandfather died in 1938 or 1939, before the Russians invaded. The Russians wouldn't have liked him because he was a businessman, trading in horses. They took people like him and sent them to Siberia.

Raising the Children

My parents were extremely successful as far as producing children. About every two years, a baby was born. I was the fourth child, the middle one. First there was Ana, then Anyeh, and then Froyem, my brother. Froyem was two years older than me. After me came my three sisters. Chayele, then Luba, then Batya. I was born in the year 1930, but the month was never clear to me.

With a big family like mine, everybody participated when a child was born. And everyone was involved with raising the children. We had a custom that a child, until the age of one and a half or two, would be swaddled in strips of sheet. A straightjacket, almost. From head to toe. My mother took a sheet, cut it into strips, sewed the strips together and rolled it all up. Wrapping the child was a major job. It took place four or five times a day. Each time the diapers were changed or the child had a bath. At that time, diapers were just a piece of cloth, so the strips of sheet had to be washed constantly. After each wrapping, the child was like a mummy. The hands were straight. The legs were straight. Toes stretched out. Only the nose and mouth were exposed, so we could see the child's face. When we picked her up, she was a stiff thing. Heavy and uncomfortable, like a bundle. Most of the time, she was put on her back. And that's where she stayed. The child was never put on her belly. She had to be watched constantly. At about a year and a half, they let the child out of those bandages so she could learn to walk. I used to question, "Why does it have to be done?"

"Lazer," I was told, "you don't want a sister with bow legs. You don't want a sister with a curved spine."

Bringing up a child was a huge amount of work. The clothes had to be scrubbed, the plates had to be washed. There were no washing machines, no dishwashers. And when children started school and came back with homework, parents had to work with them on that. Raising the children was primarily my mother's job because my father was always working, earning a living. I never saw my father change a diaper. But he baked bread. He pitched in with this and that. Neither of my parents carried water from the river once the children were old enough to do it. But I'm sure my mother got the water before we were born.

Growing up, my sisters and brother and I were respectful. No teasing going on, no fun-making. Never any fights that I recall. We had simple ways of entertaining ourselves. In warm weather, we'd take a wheel without spokes from a bicycle, and we'd take a little wooden stick and we'd run outside in the open field, banging on that rim, having a grand time. We also used to play soccer in the field. Our soccer ball was nothing but rags rolled in a ball. Rags were precious because we used them for cleaning, and if we couldn't find enough rags, our soccer ball wouldn't be full size. So we'd make a soccer ball from whatever rags we had. Tied a few strings on the outside. We'd use a couple of stones to set up a goal. Maybe three kids would play against one, but it depended on how many kids we could get to play.

I was closest to my sister Chayele. She had tremendously gorgeous looks. Big dark eyes, beautiful olive skin. Very much resembled my skin. Everybody else in the family was on the light side. From my sisters, I maintained a distance, to give them the space they needed. And my brother Froyem, I also gave him space. I would rough things up but he was calm about things, a gentle kid. Never raised his voice. Not the type of boy you'd want to give a hard time because he'd eventually cry. But I'd go out with friends and be mischievous. Froyem never did that, even though he had friends. I was more outgoing, always curious. If I finished my chores at home, I wanted to be outside exploring the landscape.

One time, I got in trouble by imitating a man chopping wood. He was a farmer who put up the fence in front of our house. He used rough-looking logs, not even cut to size. Some of them were twice the length they were supposed to be. He split the logs right on our property with a medium-sized axe held in one hand. He laid one log between two other logs and chopped away at one side. Turned it over one hundred-eighty degrees, chopped away the other side. That's how he squared off each log. One afternoon, the farmer wasn't there and he left his tools behind. I snuck out and tried to chop the wood using his technique. I was eight years old. And that axe was about as sharp as they got. I took the stance he took and chopped at the wood a couple of times. All of a sudden the axe slipped and sliced into my leg muscle close to an inch. The cut was about two inches long. My parents didn't take me to the doctor to sew it up. They just bandaged it tight and it healed well.

My father gave me a good beating for that incident. My brother never would have done such a thing. First of all, he didn't watch the farmer chop the wood the way I did. I studied how it was done. We had a pile of wood next to the house to split for the oven. And I wanted to make sure I knew how to do it. Until today, I have a scar from that axe.

In my family, children didn't show physical affection for each other. I never gave or received a hug except from my mother or father. It wasn't acceptable for children to do that. Maybe because I was dealing with girls and women. Instead, our affection was shown in everyone's behavior around the table. Today I see my grandchildren, Max and Ellie, grabbing each other, fooling around, hugging. That never went on, no. But there was a lot of sharing with my family. My mother's family, my grandfather and grandmother, sometimes came to our house for Shabbos. Sometimes we went there. We had cousins galore. My father's family wasn't around, except for one stepbrother from his mother's second marriage.

This stepbrother owned a farm outside of town. A few times over the summer, he'd invite my family to spend a day or two at the farm. They were very gracious to us. Gave us cookies and tea, showed us the animals in the barn. For some reason, this stepbrother developed a medical problem. Something minor, maybe an ulcer. Today it would be nothing. He came by wagon from his farm to the hospital in Koretz, where a doctor opened his stomach. And he died on the operating table. Over a small problem. It was unbelievable to me that he died like that. My whole family was in the hospital that morning when they took him off the wagon. Somebody must have come from his town to get us because we were family. Family was the most important thing people had.

Wolf's Work

Since my father was gifted with his hands, he did many types of work. His bicycle assembly was a thriving business. He had a middleman in another town since most of the bicycle parts came from England. Every once in a while, my father took a ride there to pick up frames and wheels and rims. He bought everything disassembled because he wanted to make money on the assembly. He planned it so the bicycles were built in wintertime since the nights were long. He'd drop off the parts in the common room and we'd sit around the stove, putting the spokes in the wheels. When they were assembled, my father sold the bikes directly. He didn't store too many. Quite a few Christians came to buy them. They'd order one in the spring when they still couldn't take it outside, because we didn't have paved roads. Most of the roads going in and out of town were just dirt. When it rained, mud was everywhere.

Aside from building bicycles, my father concentrated on his hope chest business. These were fancy painted boxes decorated in rainbow colors. Yellows, greens, reds. The type of colors people liked. My father made hinges out of brass and polished them until they sparkled. They were a big seller, these hope chests, mainly to the Christian community. When a couple got married, sometimes the family bought them a hope chest so they had a place to put their clothes. And maybe their jewelry if they had any. The size of the hope chest depended on the wealth of the family. Some of them were enormous.

My father subcontracted the carpentry and the painting of the hope chests. The carpenters did the woodwork in their homes because few people had their own shops. In summer, they worked outdoors. And in winter, they took their work into a room. The same room they slept in, they worked in. Most of it was handwork. No machinery. Many times, our home became a storage place for the hope chests, and that's why my father liked the new house. He couldn't have stored them in the house we rented. But on Manasterskya Street, he could. He brought the chests through the door and stacked up half a dozen or so along the wall. Then the painter came. He was a meticulous, slow painter. Believe me, they didn't use a sprayer back then. This was oil-based painting by hand. And the inside of the chest was shellacked so it was smooth and clean. For a long time, the fumes of the paint and shellac lingered in the house.

My father's shop was in a two-story building, walking distance from our house. It was a work space combined with living quarters. I used to go to the barber in an extended part of that building. The barber lived in the back and his store was in the front. A customer would come in, the barber would take care of his hair. Then the barber would go in back and bake some bread. My father didn't have a storefront but he was clever. He'd take a hope chest and put it on a wagon and drag it to his shop. A customer would come in and he'd show it to him. My father would say, "This is what I have."

"Well," the customer would say, "I don't like this one."

Then my father would say, "Come to my house and take a look." He would bring the customer to the house and show all the chests lined up.

"I'll take this one," the customer would say.

And they would barter about the price, because everything was bartering at that time. He'd get paid with vegetables, maybe a little money. Maybe a couple pounds of butter. When someone sold their work, they mostly got paid with goods.

The bicycle assembly and hope chest businesses were the bulk of my father's work, but he took on many other jobs. One job he had was making ornate iron fences. If somebody was building a monument in the cemetery and wanted to enclose it with an iron fence, he'd come to my father. My father had the means of fabricating iron in his shop. He'd buy the iron and get a blacksmith. The blacksmith would do the heavy work and my father would do the fine work. And he'd make a stunning iron fence.

Another job my father did was make hardware for people who were building a custom window or a custom door in their home. Special locks and latches, that's what he made.

He also had a safe assembly business. We had several banks in town, and my father was the one who serviced the safes. Men who hunted in the winter came to my father for the animal traps he built. Some of those traps were huge. God forbid if a horse stepped in one. Those traps would take its leg right off. These hunters killed animals for their skins. They were mostly gentiles but a couple of Jews were trappers, too. Some Jews were in the fur business and they traded, like our neighbor on Manasterskya Street, who traded in skins and shoe leather.

My father was also talented with fixing sewing machines. Farmers didn't have any means of bringing their sewing machines to my father, so my father went to them. In those days, sewing machines were not compact. The top of the sewing machine was bulky, and on the bottom there was a treadle for the feet. My father would get on his bike and when I was about five or six years old, I would go with him. I'd sit on the frame of his bike and he'd pedal a few miles out of town. He'd bring his tools in a little bag. Usually spend three or four hours fixing a sewing machine, then get paid with goods.

When I was seven, my father brought me on a particular job to repair a sewing machine. He was hired by a devoted Christian family five miles from Koretz. They came and transported us by wagon. By our standards, they had a substantial farm. The family was not large, just the father and mother and four kids. They grew potatoes and the way they preserved them from season to season was by burying them in deep holes.

My father's work extended a bit late in the afternoon and still he wasn't finished. He decided we'd spend the night there so he could finish the job and wouldn't have to return. It was mainly, I think, that he wanted to get paid for his work. I asked, "Why do we have to stay overnight and sleep in their house?" There was no way of informing my family we weren't coming home. They might be worried. But my father made his decision and there was no discussion. Keep in mind, I wasn't questioning his authority. It was more that I was afraid of spending a night with a Christian family in a little farm town where we didn't know anybody. There was a fear we had being among Christians. Maybe the townspeople knew about us. But my father was brave and said, "Lazer, we're going to finish the job. We'll have supper and spend the night here."

Supper consisted of a lot of potatoes. Soup made out of potatoes. Boiled potatoes, mashed potatoes. Some sour cream. Lots of bread. We ate so much starch, I didn't want to see another potato. After supper, my father worked late into the night by primitive lights. Remember, the light in those days was nothing but a kerosene lamp. Early in the morning, my father woke me up, around three a.m. The family brought us back by wagon to our house. By the time the sun came up, we were home. Evidently my father had other work he had to be back for, so that job ended well.

This was the type of trip my father brought me on. I don't think he ever asked my brother Froyem to accompany him. First of all, Froyem wouldn't have wanted to go. He never minded that I went, though. I knew it was an adventurous thing I did with my dad. Never before had I left my family and spent a night in a Christian house. But I didn't brag about it. I talked about the food we ate. How it was plentiful, but too many potatoes.

My dad and I took other trips later on. The war years were extremely dangerous. But my father had trust in me. He knew I had the strength to go places with him. I was small and thin but fast, considered a healthy child. Most of those trips involved a great deal of walking. Many places, my father wouldn't take a bike, since it was a material possession. A bike was something that somebody might want, no matter how old it was. During the war years, people would kill for a bike. If his customer couldn't provide transportation, he'd walk. He carried his tools in a bag. Then the worst that could happen was someone would want his tools. And it could happen. Some of those guys would have killed for shoelaces.

When I was nine years old, my father built a dental press for a dentist, to make crowns out of gold or steel. That was a stylish thing. If a tooth fell out, people wanted a crown. Today when a patient needs a dental crown, the dentist gives a technician the measurements and the mold, and the technician makes it for him. But back then, dentists had to do everything themselves. They wanted a bridge, they had to make it. They wanted a crown, they had to go and make it.

This dentist came to my father and asked him to make not just one or two, but to make a crown for every tooth in the mouth. It became quite a job for my father. The press was the same, but the shape of each tooth was, of course, unique. After all, front teeth look different than back teeth. My father needed a means to design the shape of each tooth. I'll never forget that this dentist brought over not individual teeth, but a whole mouth with teeth. The jawbone and everything. He took it out of a cadaver. The bone had to be preserved or else it would start smelling. So the dentist put it in some sort of solution. And my father would open it up from the jar and work on each tooth separately. He'd measure it and make the cavity and make the core to press it in. The job took a couple of months during the winter. After my father finished, he delivered the press to the dentist in early spring.

The dentist soon needed a few adjustments to the press, so he dropped it off for my father to work on. He let my father have it only for a couple of hours because he needed it back right away. My father did some filing, did some fixing, and it was done. When I came from school that day, my father told me to carry the press to the dentist. The dentist's house wasn't far from our house, maybe a quarter mile. I knew where he lived because I was friends with his son. I carried the press carefully, up to his big house with a wrought iron fence, which showed that this dentist had the means. I walked to the door past soft, green grass. The dentist had a small dog and I don't know what breed it was, but that dog went after me. He came running and barking at me with sharp teeth. I was wearing short pants because it was a warm day. And the dog really chewed my leg. I held onto the dental press until finally I got too scared and dropped it. Luckily it fell on the grass, because the dentist had a red brick walkway. I said to myself, "Lazer, don't drop the press on the walkway because it will get damaged." My father was busy on other projects and I knew he didn't want to work anymore on the press, especially since he was already paid.

Well, that dentist came out of the house and he started yelling at me. My leg was bleeding and I was shaking. I said, "It's not my fault the dog doesn't like me." Then I ran to the shop and showed my leg to my dad. My dad left everything and went to the dentist to see what happened. I stayed in the shop. When my dad came back, he didn't say a word. He didn't complain. Apparently he got the story that I didn't provoke the dog. In those days, if you provoked something, you sure got punished. But everything worked out that time.

My father was known in Koretz for the work he did. But outside of work, his role in the community was limited. He mostly went to shul and associated with his family. At that time, there were political committees and Zionist groups in Koretz, but my father never joined those committees. He avoided politics. There were also committees associated with the shul, but my father didn't get involved with those, either. Mainly he had a large family to take care of. He had many chores and they took time. You know, most people didn't go out and buy their bread. They baked it. We had stores, but few people bought things. Most people had to be industrious. Whenever my father had extra time, he picked up some work here and there or connected with a customer. Then he packed up his tools and came home.

The Community of Koretz

When I was a boy, Koretz was a thriving Jewish community. There was a Jewish population close to six thousand, and two thousand gentiles. The Jewish people in Koretz went back many, many generations. We had our own cemetery that was close to a thousand years old. Before the war, most Jews had their own small shops. Trades of all kinds. There were tailors, butchers and barbers. Some were blacksmiths, catering to farmers. They shoed horses and fixed the farmers' wagons. We had shoemakers who made tall leather boots that were popular. They catered to the Jewish community and also to the gentiles in surrounding farms. Several shoemakers bought leather from our neighbor who traded in animal skins. Just a few miles from the Russian border was a prosperous sugar factory in Koretz, where sugar was extracted from sugar beets. Some Jews worked there.

The mills in Koretz were primitive. Take the saw mill. In those days, people started from scratch to make boards for building barns or furniture. The saw mill was nothing more than a platform where one guy stayed on top and there was a big, powerful saw on the bottom. The blade was about six feet long. They marked a line on top, marked a line on the bottom, and that was how they cut boards. I used to go and watch them.

The flour mill was the biggest factory in town, owned by a couple of wealthy brothers. They provided flour for all of Koretz, as well as for many little towns nearby. At their flour mill, the grain was stored on the outside. Inside there were two flat rocks, about six feet in diameter, with a hole in the middle. A worker would take a pail of grain and pour the grain in the hole. There was a block of wood that caught the stone on top, with a horse on one side and a horse on the other side. They trotted in a circle. One pulled this way and the other pulled the other way. And that was how they ground flour. Every once in a while, the workers emptied the flour out of one pail while the horses were still moving. They ran to catch the other pail and spilled the flour, because the mechanism never stopped. Those horses went for half a day. When they were switched with another pair of horses, the workers drank water and quickly fed themselves. Then a different pair of horses trotted around for another five hours. I used to go and watch that, too.

The same method was used to make oil from poppy seeds. It was a simple way of life. The sophisticated places used water power because the Korchyk River had plenty of water. They worked a stream of water using an enormous wheel. Some factories used wind power, but they had to depend on the wind, which didn't always work. Horses always worked, winter and summer. In early 1938 when electricity came to town, several mills switched over to electrical power. The brothers that owned the flour mill got electricity at their plant.

The town of Koretz changed hands many times. In 1930 it was part of Poland, and now it's a part of the Ukraine. No matter what government was in power, the primary language of the Jews was Yiddish. That was the language we spoke at home. We also spoke Polish and Ukrainian, so we could get along with our neighbors. In 1939, when the Russians came in, we were forced to learn Russian, so we spoke a variety of languages.

Although Koretz was primarily Jewish, the administration of the town was gentile, mainly of Polish descent. Life was pretty good for the Jews as I recall. Sure, we had anti-Semitism prior to the war, but we always had anti-Semitism. We had times during the year when hooligans would raise hell. And there were pogroms that took place but I don't recall them firsthand. I felt anti-Semitism when I was at public school, and my father felt anti-Semitism all the time, but it was something we got used to living with.

Jews and gentiles mostly lived in separate parts of town, but some were mixed in together. A Christian man lived not too far from my grandfather's house. And there was a sausage factory that belonged to a well-established gentile family near our house. This same family was also in charge of security, Koretz's police force. So there was intermingling. There were periods of time when the Jews and the Christians got along but most of the time the Christians got inflamed about things. Maybe stuff about the Jews was said in church. Maybe things were said at home. Who knows?

This was the type of thing that happened. A Christian boy would beat up a Jewish boy for no reason, even though they were friends.

The Jewish boy would say, "We were just playing. How come you're beating me up?"

"Well, I learned that you Jews killed Jesus Christ. That's why I'm beating you up."

These families were so ignorant. They didn't know any history. The Jewish boy got beaten because the Christian boy was learning anti-Semitism. There was such terrible animosity and no one knew why. You would think a Christian nun wouldn't behave this way. We had a convent in town. The nuns dressed a certain way, they walked a certain way. They were proper ladies. But their attitude toward us was one of hatred. They themselves participated in the beatings. It's hard to imagine that anti-Semitism was so widespread, so acceptable. But there it was.

As far as the Jewish community was concerned, the cultural aspect of Koretz was quite strong. We had a Jewish theater and a couple of Jewish newspapers that advertised the shows. There was ongoing talk about famous Jewish writers like Bialyk, who wrote in Yiddish, of course. We had a well-organized Zionist movement, which inspired many Jews from Koretz to emigrate to Palestine in the 1920s and 1930s. We had a library in town, but we never went there. Children were not taken to the library like they are today. There was a private club in Koretz with a clay tennis court where we watched tennis matches. We had a traveling soccer team, too. That was a big thing. And there was a movie theater, though the tickets were expensive. I saw my first movie when I was seven or eight years old. It was a Hollywood film that had something to do with trains and cowboys, an action movie. My first impression of America. A few minutes before the movie, a newsreel blasted away about world events.

The public schools went all the way through college. There were several Hebrew schools as well. We had one major shul and it wasn't cheap to belong there. And there were smaller shuls. My family affiliated with the shul that my grandparents on my mother's side belonged to. Because they were segregated, the women sat on one side and the men sat on the other. Froyem and my father and I sat next to my grandfather Avram.

Koretz was also a historic town. There was an old, brick fortress next to the police station. One of my favorite places. Under tall, shady trees, people would bring a picnic in the summer. The popular sport in that park was shooting crows. That was the hobby of policemen and other gentiles in law enforcement who carried guns. I watched them shoot at the crows and it tore me up inside. There were these spectacular birds flying so freely and nesting in the trees. Then all of a sudden they were shot down. Hunted and killed. Never just chased away.

Aside from the fortress, the other historic place in town was the cemetery. The cemetery was on a hill, away from the Korchyk River. But there was a clear spring at the bottom of the hill where the water was delicious. Clean and cold, summer and winter. We used to wash our hands there. And the story we used to tell was the water came from people who were buried in the cemetery. They were peeing.

As I said, my family went to the Korchyk River to get water, but some parts of town had a common well. People would drop a pail down and roll it up full of water. Mind you, those wooden pails weighed a ton when they were filled. The wells were only about fifteen or twenty feet deep. They were convenient in good weather, but in wintertime, they were frozen solid.

Winters were harsh, no doubt about it. Traveling in or out of Koretz was a real production when it snowed. Farmers would come to town in bulky, homemade sleds. The rest of the year, farmers came by horse and wagon. In the summer, those who could afford it rode a bike. Most people did a lot of walking. There were certain days in warm weather when we'd walk barefoot because we were saving our shoes.

In 1937, travel improved quite a bit. A bus company was established and it became easier for people to commute to different places. To do business, to visit friends. Some had family in other cities and would travel back and forth. Some went to other towns for schooling and different types of education. Those who could afford it. It wasn't that expensive, but you needed the few coins to buy a ticket.

Education

My father and mother had minimal education. Maybe fourth-grade public schooling. But everybody in our house knew how to read and write. My father wrote letters in Yiddish to his mother, to his sisters in Argentina, to his sister in Zhytomyr. He also wrote in Polish. Education back then was mostly focused on the male part of the family. It's not that my father or mother were discriminating. They were concentrating to make sure the males of the family would have the proper tools to become providers, because women in those days were homemakers. None of my sisters were sent to learn Hebrew, whereas Froyem and I were. None of my sisters were reprimanded when they didn't spend time doing their homework. But Froyem and I were constantly questioned by my father and mother. "You done your homework?"

Before I started first grade, I was taught to read Hebrew and Yiddish by a rabbi. He was not a rabbi that ran a shul. He was more like a teacher, a learned man. He taught me the Hebrew alphabet and Jewish law and customs through the Torah. I went to his house and sat for private lessons that lasted an hour and a half. Sometimes two hours. He taught me everything. How to pray, how to use a prayer book, Hebrew songs, pronunciations, preparation for bar mitzvah. He would shake and yell if I didn't concentrate. Being tutored was common in those days. I used to go to him three or four times a week. After the fourth or fifth lesson, when he felt he knew me, this rabbi spent a lot of time cleaning and trimming his nails while he was teaching. He'd clip his nails with a knife and put the clippings into a little steel box. Maybe he did this so he wouldn't have to drop the nail clippings on the floor. He was a pious man.

A lot of wealthy farmers brought their children to public school in Koretz because that was the only way they'd get an education. The majority of farmers didn't educate their children. They were illiterate. But the farmers that had the means, they transported their children. Mind you, that was a job. There was no school bus like there is today. Those farmers put their kids on a horse and buggy and brought them to town.

I was seven when I started public school and I attended for four years, until the Germans invaded. There were thirty children in my class with one teacher. We sat close together on a bench attached to a table, no more than sixteen inches wide. There was a lot of looking back and forth. It was hard to learn under those conditions. None of us had any fun. At school there was no playground, no recreation. And it was a loose structure as far as what we were taught. For weeks at a time, we practiced writing letters of the alphabet. Or we practiced multiplication tables over and over. The teacher would say, "Write a page of As, or write a page of Bs." For arithmetic, we'd write numbers. The curriculum was not there, not like it is today. The teacher never had enough books so we used to share them. But the teacher chose who was going to bring the book home. Many times she wouldn't let students take a book if she thought it wasn't going to come back.

We called it public school but it was actually parochial school run by the Catholic Church. The Polish people were devoted Catholics and the school went through the mass on a daily basis. A lot of time was taken up with prayers. Us Jewish kids used to stand and look at the ceiling. Didn't say a word. Just stood there and listened. And it was uncomfortable. A lot of Jewish kids didn't go there because of that atmosphere. They went to *Tarbut*, the Hebrew school. When I began school, about a third of the students in my class were Jewish. Maybe half a dozen Jewish children out of twenty, twenty-four kids. But over time, Jewish families withdrew their children and sent them to Tarbut. By the end, only a handful of students were Jewish. I was picked on from time to time because I was one of them. Sometimes Christian bullies would gang up on me. There was no one to complain to.

The town's nunnery was adjacent to the school and when our teacher didn't show up, the nuns appeared. They had ceremonies. They told us how Jesus suffered on the cross. The nuns were not interested in teaching anything other than religion. There were two pictures on the wall. A picture of the president of Poland, and next to it, a picture of Jesus Christ. When the nun showed up in my class, she pointed to Jesus Christ and said, "You're going to Hell if you don't do this, if you don't do that." And the kids took it seriously. They were affected by that. I used to come home and complain, say that I wanted to go to a different school. But it didn't happen.

My father wanted to stay away from politics and the Jewish schools were affiliated with political parties. Some were to the left, some were to the right. My father didn't want to get involved with that. The Jewish schools were doing the opposite of what the Catholic schools did. They wanted you to be Zionist. They wanted you to align yourself with the Jewish people and go to Palestine, the Jewish homeland. They wanted you to think about socialism. When the Russians took over, the Hebrew schools disappeared. They didn't believe in private school, in Jewish education. So they closed them. But until 1939, there were three or four well-attended Hebrew schools in Koretz.

My brother Froyem wanted to go to Tarbut so badly. The same school as his friends. But my father told Froyem, "You're going to public school like everybody else." All my siblings went to public school like me. But my brother hated it most of all. I know he had a taste of Tarbut from his buddies. I didn't have friends that went to Tarbut. But I did have some friends among the gentile kids at public school. And with those kids, religion was not an issue. We were just kids at school together. I interacted with them and was respectful of what they did. I didn't mix in their business and we got along. Nobody invited me to church, but a lot of Jewish kids did get invited. In fact, some Jews from Koretz converted to Catholicism because their children went to the public school and made friends. But the war years weren't any easier for those families. Because once the Germans came, conversion didn't mean a thing.

The Russian Invasion

We didn't have advanced warning when the Russians invaded in September of 1939. We saw one or two Russian planes fly over Koretz earlier that day, then they showed up in a massive representation as far as soldiers and guns and tanks. We should have had plenty of warning because we were right on the Russian border. The first to get hit. But they stormed in and no one was prepared. Some people cheered in the street but most people stayed away. My parents told us not to leave the house. The Russian army came in with a bang and took over the town. They put the fear into us.

The influx of troops went on for months, pouring through Koretz. It took weeks and weeks for the Russians to move because most of them were on foot. There was one main cobblestone road in Koretz that led to Rovno and all the little towns in between. The other roads were just dirt. That wasn't efficient for the Russians. First thing, they formed a paramilitary to build a railroad so they could bring in more soldiers. They rounded up the young, able men, put them in black uniforms and gave them hats and boots. Day and night these men worked, three and four shifts a day. They set up a canteen in town where they fed them. The Russians made a big deal about the paramilitary and tried to recruit more men. They used propaganda and people bought into it.

Men came from all over because conditions were tough. Food and clothing were scarce. There was no money. And it wasn't clear how people should behave. Nobody knew what was allowed under Russian communism.

A lot of Jews joined the paramilitary. Most of the recruits were sent to Russia to build railroads. Some were left behind in Koretz. I don't know how many miles they built a day, but that railroad line to Rovno was built quickly and soon I saw trains for the first time. They carried soldiers and weapons. I used to watch them go by.

Their tanks, compared to today, were small and primitive. They moved them by the thousands. The dirt roads of Koretz were chewed up by such heavy traffic. When it rained, the muddy surface slowed them down. So the Russians started to pave the roads with tar. On a daily basis, I used to run to the center of town and watch them pave. There was one thing about that project that surprised all of us. It was quite involved to pave the main road through the center of town. They could have easily built a road outside of town, bypassed the river, and still connected to Rovno, the next city. That would have been a much simpler way of doing things. The town didn't need extra traffic going through it. But they did it their way.

While they were paving, the Russians decided to replace the bridge crossing the Korchyk River. The original wooden bridge was built years before but the wood couldn't hold up to moving tanks and heavy equipment. So they mobilized the local people in the paramilitary and had them rebuild the bridge. Again they worked around the clock. At night, they set up lights that were powered by a generator. Under these conditions, the bridge was rebuilt using steel and cement.

Next the Russians built a landing for planes outside of town, in the pastures. Their air force wasn't too powerful. No heavy fighters, no heavy bombers. Mostly they had biplanes. They weren't that sophisticated but we were impressed. Many kids went to the pastures and watched the planes land and take off. Most of them had a machine gun attached to them. They didn't have any means of dropping bombs.

All of this activity took place in 1939 and 1940. The Russians came in with such power. They installed their own government and mayor, and told the locals that Poland was under Russian rule. They made sure there would be no free enterprise. They took most of the big wheels that were running businesses and, without any charges, these people disappeared. The undesirables were the wealthy people. No trials for them. Nothing. One day they were gone and nobody ever saw them again. We thought they were sent to Siberia. But who knows? They might have been taken to another town and shot.

My dad immediately changed the way he was doing business. He could no longer hire people and make money off them because that was capitalism. Taking advantage of people. Not the Russian way. My father quickly realized it was a system you better live by, otherwise you would die by it. First, he eliminated his hope chest business, which was a large part of his income. He became a one-man show and tried to make a living on his own. He was curtailed, his income was hurting. But he was in relatively good shape. We had our house and he was self-sustained. My family managed. I can't say our standard of living was so bad. The families that owned capital-intensive businesses, like flour mills and oil factories, they were greatly affected. We were not.

Everything changed under the Russians. Religion was frowned on. People still prayed, but not to the extent they prayed before. Kind of disguised. Not as open. We went to shul in a quiet manner, but a lot of people were afraid to go. Tarbut, the Jewish school system, was closed down. The Zionist movement went underground. The people involved in Jewish theater, they stopped performing because theater wasn't supposed to take place. Other changes, too. There was no more marketplace. The open-air market where people bought and sold vegetables, sometimes sold old clothing and shoes and furniture, well, that was taking advantage of people. So it ended.

The Russians promoted public executions, mainly to scare people. It was a reminder of what would happen if you continued your involvement with things from the past. The authorities would make everyone go out and witness the executions. Most people didn't want to watch. But they were forced. Children and sick people, everybody. They scared the hell out of us. It was a very depressing situation for grown-ups. Children, they adapt to things. We took it with a grain of salt. This was life.

The Russians publicized large families and there was an explosion of birth rates. They encouraged mothers to give birth in the hospital. Medicine was free, doctors were free. The more children people had, they were exempt from certain taxes. Maybe they were compensated for extra children. My father and mother brought my sister Batya into the world at that time. I don't know if she evolved because there were some perks to having another child. The Russians tried to make communism appealing.

Another thing they pushed was athletics. In 1940, they organized a mini-marathon. It was about five kilometers, maybe even ten. The first time I ran in a road race, and I went barefoot. I didn't make the whole distance because I was too young. But I participated because I was encouraged to do that.

People frowned about the Russian takeover but nobody talked about it. Everybody was afraid. You didn't trust your neighbors. You didn't know their political leanings. There was no free discussion going on, no casual exchanges among townspeople. At home, too, there was little discussion about what was happening. Before the Russians came, we used to sit and talk openly about everything on Friday nights, but that completely stopped. It's amazing what a political system can do to a family. Parents were afraid their children would pick up something at home and talk about it with their friends. We didn't know if we were saying the right things. Even our record player was silent. We didn't know what music to play or even if that equipment was appropriate. We were learning what we should know, whether we liked it or not.

School actually improved under the Russians. I went to the same school with a different curriculum. We were taught Russian and we picked it up quickly because it's a Slavic language. The morning prayers, they stopped. And the pictures on the walls, including the crucifixes, they disappeared. It was more of a progressive education. The Russians concentrated on the young. They tried to grab young minds. Because young people were their future.

The Russians ignored older people because they were set in their ways. Or the Russians taught them a lesson by executing them. There wasn't much the Russians would tolerate. There would be a short court session and boom! They were gone. The people who disappeared weren't associates of my father. I'm quite sure if my father had any such aquaintances, then he'd have been affected, too. They didn't leave people alone. If a man was associated with an undesirable, then everyone was involved. This was true for both gentiles and Jews.

There was no resistance to the Russians. No fighting at all. The Russians moved about freely, any place they wanted to go. The Polish army was not that strong, barely equipped. I don't know if the Polish army even had any planes. It was surprising to us how many people within our Jewish community believed in the Russian system. Quite a few Jews became involved with managing town offices. I don't know where these people were before. Came out of the woodwork. They were Bolsheviks and supported the communist cause. They also tried to impose their lifestyle on everybody. Many people wished the Bolsheviks would cross the Russian border and be on the other side.

The Russians needed places to sleep, of course. The average soldiers slept in the street. Set up a tent here or there. Sometimes they took over small buildings. Or they found an open field and slept there. They were not that sophisticated. The generals or captains, on the other hand, availed themselves of people's homes. Just moved in with a family. Somebody of authority would move in, take over a room in a house, set up an office. That was their system. It didn't happen to us, but it happened to a lot of people. These soldiers walked in and stayed. And mind you, the homes were not that big. The Russians didn't kick the people out, though. They were looking to recruit.

My family didn't have direct interaction with the authorities. Everybody kept their distance. We, as children, just went to school, minded our own business. Came home. We were excited about some of the happenings because they were new. We talked about it among ourselves. Things were different. Life was really changing.

In 1940, my father brought my oldest sister Ana to Zhytomyr in Russia, to visit his sister. Prior to that, there was limited access to Russia. But under the occupation, it was much easier to cross the border. When my father and Ana came back, they talked very little. My siblings and I asked them a lot of questions, of course, after such a big trip. "What type of home does our aunt have? Does she have a better lifestyle than us?" After all, she and her family had been under the Russian regime all their lives. We asked questions but few answers came back. I had the sense my father wasn't impressed with life in Russia. Maybe he told my mother about that trip, but he didn't talk to us children about it. We knew my mother's side of the family because most of them were in Koretz and we saw them frequently. But this was my father's side. We never met any of his relatives, aside from his stepbrother. This aunt was his only family in Russia. I'm quite sure my father invited his sister and her family but they never visited Koretz. Maybe she didn't have the means to make it happen. We always questioned this. After all, family was important to us.

By the spring of 1941, we knew about Hitler and the Germans in the western part of Europe, but it wasn't discussed openly. In those days, a few people had radios but the primary means of communication was telegraph. That's how knowledge got around. My family never got a telegram, but us children heard grown-ups exchange words about what was happening. A couple of months before the German invasion, there was quite a bit of commotion. Jewish refugees were stopping by our house on their way to Russia, looking for a drink of water, a quick place to rest. They talked about atrocities that were taking place but nobody wanted to believe what they said about the Germans. My father fed them bread, gave them a drink. They stayed for a short time and took off.

Things were quiet for a while, until immediately before the Germans invaded. Suddenly, dozens of Jews stopped in Koretz and asked for water and food. Resupplied themselves. Most of them were on foot. Many people that had the means of transportation wasted their time debating whether or not they should flee. The refugees told us about the killings and brutalities. We listened but we didn't leave. We had little food, no means, no transportation. No place to go with a family of nine.

Around this time, my mother's brother, Uncle Yosef, took off for Russia with his family. He had four children and a goat. When they were leaving, Uncle Yosef told my father he should come to the house and take the goat, which he did. We kept the goat in our house and drank its milk. When food grew scarce, my father found a shochet, who slaughtered the goat in return for some meat. We had a few decent meals and shared the meat with our neighbors. Meat doesn't stay too long.

All the while, the Germans were moving closer. We didn't know how far into the territory the Germans had advanced, whether they reached Rovno or other places. We were in the dark. The Russians and the Germans didn't want us to know too much. What nobody knew was that Hitler and Stalin had made a secret pact to divide Poland, but Hitler broke the agreement. He wanted Poland for himself. The Russian occupation lasted two years until the Germans kicked them out. In the summer of 1941. Oh yes, I have memories of that. It happened overnight.

The German Invasion

German troops entered Koretz on July 2, 1941. Two planes showed up that night and dropped half a dozen bombs on the town. My whole family left the house. We ran through a narrow passage that led to the Korchyk River. It was a rainy, slippery night. There was lightning. We found ourselves in a little ditch on the riverbank. Most of the bombs hit the center of Koretz. They weren't big bombs, but we saw high explosions. Overall, there was little damage. Might have been a few craters. Maybe they hit a truck driving back to Russia. The Russians were in retreat. We saw thousands and thousands and thousands of Russian soldiers marching toward the border. Begging for a glass of water. They'd been kicked, beaten down. So many soldiers. But very little equipment going back. They were probably marched to some place and then shot.

The Germans came in fast and killed anybody who stood in their way. A couple of streets from us lived a Jewish man in a two-story house. The Germans hung him from his balcony on the second floor. They left him hanging for almost a week. We kept asking ourselves, "Why? Why? Why?" The Germans exerted their authority so brutally. They were more advanced than the Russians in their assaults, in their weaponry. We saw dozens and dozens of German planes flying above Koretz, moving toward Russia.

The Germans were also more skillful at feeding their soldiers. I used to walk to certain places in town and watch them prepare meals. They killed anything they found. Goats. Chickens. Cows. A lot of townspeople raised chickens and kept goats for milk. The Germans took what they wanted. Or they went outside the town, grabbed a cow and slaughtered it. I saw that many times. They had portable kitchens to feed their army. Yes, the Germans were quite prepared. And they were unstoppable. It didn't take long before we understood what was really happening. They encouraged the local Christian community to get rid of the Jews. Told them to attack us. The Germans asked the town to elect people to represent the Jewish community. Then they instantly killed them. Got rid of the Jewish leadership. We knew right then and there we were fighting for our lives.

Soon they made us wear *Mogen Davids,* Jewish stars made of yellow cloth. I don't know where we got the yellow material. We had to sew them on the front and back of our clothing. Clearly sewn so everyone could see. They had to be a certain size, close to five inches in diameter. My family, my aunts and uncles and cousins, we were all affected. Uncle

Yosef was lucky that he fled before the invasion. After the Germans showed up, nobody could leave.

The first big killing took place in August of 1941. The Germans came with their helpers, the Christians. These were men and women we knew, townspeople and neighbors. The Christians helped round up young men between the ages of seventeen and thirty. They were looking for a certain number of them. If they didn't get that number, they took older men. They rounded up more than three hundred men that day.

They took Uncle Menashe, my mother's brother. He was hiding but somehow they got him out of the house. He lived not far from our grandmother. He had a family, four children. I watched them put these young men on a truck. And I ran and ran after the truck to see where it went. I saw Uncle Menashe on the truck and I raced home to tell my mother about it. She tried to calm us down. Told us they were looking for people to take them to work. But there was no work. Those guys were never coming back. They took those three hundred men outside of town and shot them. Uncle Menashe was the first from the family to be killed.

A few months later, there were plans for another slaughter. We knew something terrible was about to happen because everyone was talking. The Christians that came from outside Koretz informed the townspeople that huge mass graves were being dug in a forest area called Kozak. Local Christians were digging the graves by hand. It took them a couple of weeks because even though the soil was sandy and soft, the graves were enormous. They were six feet deep and one hundred twenty-five feet long by seventy-five feet wide. Word came into town when the two mass graves were finished. It was the spring of 1942. We were expecting something awful. We waited. Had no place to go.

Early one morning at about five a.m., we heard banging on the door. The windows were crashing. Two Germans were yelling at us to get out of the house. Right away my father started screaming at everybody to hide. There were pre-arranged places for hiding, most of them in the attic. This was kind of stupid because everybody knew there was an attic in the house. The ladder was there already because my father had prepared in advance. While the banging went on, my mother and my older sisters Ana and Anyeh took Batya, the baby, and my younger sister Luba. They climbed into the attic and lifted the ladder up after them. They pulled a cover across the attic entrance. I was in the bedroom with Froyem and my little sister Chayeleh, huddled under the bed. The Germans broke down the door and saw us there. They dragged the three of us outside. We weren't doing a good job hiding. My father was dragged out of the house, too.

We stood in front of our house on Manasterskya Street. Me, my father, Froyem and Chayeleh. The Germans were rounding up our neighbors and bringing them to the front of our house as well. They were gathering us so they could march us off together. I stood behind my father. Remember, he was a big, stocky man. He started pushing me with his elbow and he said in Yiddish, "Get away from here." But I didn't know where to go. There was no place to escape. I saw Germans banging on the dentist's door and the dentist's daughter jumped out her second floor window. She was my sister Ana's age, seventeen years old. The German standing in front of me and my father aimed his rifle at the girl.

While he was shooting at her, I snuck around the back of the house and crawled into the outhouse. There was a small window there. I didn't see the rest of my family. Of course, they were in the attic. I stayed there until I saw my father and Chayeleh and Froyem marched away, along with our neighbors. After a while, my mother lifted up a ceramic tile on the roof. She peeked out and saw there were no Germans in front of the house anymore. The street had been cleaned up. All was quiet. I snuck from the outhouse to the house and whispered I was downstairs. My mother and sisters opened the attic lid and lowered the ladder. I climbed upstairs to the attic and clung to them. We stayed there the whole day.

We had so many black crows that day. I never saw so many in my life. They kept on flying across the sky. I said Ana and Anyeh, "Why can't I be this crow? So I can fly through the air, so I can fly away." Why were the crows there? There was some reason. The sky was full of them. So much cawing and squawking.

Later that night, my father came back, though he was alone. He told us what happened after he and Chayeleh and Froyem and my neighbors were marched away. Two German soldiers and two Christian locals with rifles guarded the group. They passed an orchard my father was familiar with. And at that point, he ran for the woods. It wasn't that thick an orchard and the Germans let off a couple shots after him. My father ducked the bullets and found himself lying in a ravine outside the orchard. He survived the day there. Late at night, the shooting stopped. No more noise. My father worked his way up from where he was and snuck back to the house. We were still hiding in the attic. He called to us and we climbed down. We saw that Chayeleh and Froyem weren't with him. There were a lot of tears. He hugged us in his damp, dirty clothes. All of us crying.

We didn't spend that night at home. We stayed outside near the river. There we felt more secure. The next day was May 22, 1942, and we learned the Germans had rounded up 2,200 Jews. Chayeleh and Froyem were taken to Kozak and killed at the mass graves with everyone else.

A few days later, the locals allowed the Jews to go to the graves and fill them in. They were barely covered with dirt. We didn't have other transportation, so we walked. My father and I carried shovels. Kozak wasn't far, just five or seven miles from town. We could have easily been killed on that trip, but the locals didn't hassle us.

At the edge of the forest, the wind carried a foul odor. Farmers came up to us and told us what happened. There were two mass graves. One for men, the other for women and children. The Jews were made to undress. Leave their clothes in a pile. As soon as they were naked, they were marched to the sandy graves. A German soldier with a pistol shot a bullet in each of them. In the back of their heads.

As my father and I shoveled the yellow dirt onto the graves, I felt the soft ground giving beneath my feet. The corpses were just six or twelve inches underneath me. Knowing that Chayele and Froyem were in that grave was overwhelming. The shovel was heavy and my hands were shaking. Chayeleh was just ten years old. A little gypsy girl with olive skin and curly hair. Froyem, shy and gentle at fourteen. Dirt was in our shoes, on our clothes. My mother couldn't stop crying.

The Ghetto

When we came back from the graves, the surviving Jews were forced into a ghetto. The authorities sectioned off a couple of streets, just a few blocks from our home. Close to the cemetery. That part of town was easier for them to control. We took over an empty house where Jews had been killed. And we were kept in that ghetto with the other remaining Jews. Trapped like rats. Forbidden to leave.

In the ghetto, life turned on the bad end. Things got much, much worse. We had only a few clothes and my father's tool bag. The rest of our possessions were at Manasterskya Street. Of course, we couldn't return there. The biggest problem was the shortage of food. We were still a large family even though we lost two children. Five children needed to be fed. And there was no food to be seen anyplace. One day my father came in with an egg. It was a big decision how we were going to divide it. After some discussion, my mother concocted a dish where she utilized the egg. So everyone could have a bite of protein.

One or two Jews in the ghetto had some means. And they shared those means with the rest of us. People pitched in what they had. If a family had a bag of flour, they'd make a fire, bake some bread, and share that bread with everyone else. If a man had a coin in his pocket, he'd contribute. If he had nothing to give, that was okay. He could have a piece of bread and wouldn't owe a thing. There was nothing more we could do for each other. Everything was very strict, very tense. There was no light talk, no song. Children, husbands, wives had been murdered before our eyes.

Koretz still had an influx of refugees. Jews were sneaking toward the Russian border, hoping to bypass the German front lines and escape. But no matter where they fled, they were going to be dead. Almost on a nightly basis, we had people stop by our house with swollen feet, blisters, hardly any shoes. They didn't have proper clothing. They were walking for who knows how long. Most of these people came from places we never heard of. They talked about the killings, about the violence. But they made it through. They made it to a little town at night. Hopefully, they'd get a glass of water and maybe even a slice of bread in the ghetto. They tried to comfort themselves and they tried to comfort us. Told us what was coming. They said, "If you stick around here, you'll be killed." Most of them were young people, traveling by moonlight. There were no maps. No directions. Who knew if they were traveling the right road?

As a family, because of our size, we could do nothing. No food, no transportation, nowhere to go. We were stuck in that ghetto, sitting and waiting for our deaths. But the bottom line was that none of us blamed anybody. That's what really surprised me about the whole thing. I never remember my mother saying to my father, or we as children saying, "Daddy should have known better." Nobody complained. Everybody stuck together, doing what we could.

While we were in the ghetto, my father concentrated on finding hiding places for us. He turned to his Christian customers. The ones he trusted. Someone he sold a hope chest to, or somebody he fixed a sewing machine for. He didn't have that close a relationship with too many people, but in a situation like this, my father extended himself. It was like we were sinking in a river. He reached out to any branch that might save our lives.

Before sunrise, my father and I would sneak out of the ghetto. Get up early, when it was dark. Walk for miles into the countryside. Look for hiding places, look for some bread. A strong man with a boy at his side. We'd visit his customers' homes and try to walk out with something to eat. "Could you give us a loaf of bread or some potatoes?" He asked but never begged. And if we were lucky, we wound up with some food. Those customers, they remembered him. They couldn't do much to help us. If not food, they'd give ideas about where to go.

On the way back from one trip, an amputee approached us on horseback. He had a wooden leg and carried a rifle. He acted like he was part of the militia because he had a weapon. But he didn't look that sophisticated. It was probably a gun he used for hunting deer. He came right behind us and asked, "Who are you?" He started talking to my father and accused him of being Jewish.

"Judea." Judea was a word they used for describing a Jew. "You're a Jew."

My father was edgy because the guy was on a horse and had a weapon, so he had the power. My father told him he was in the area looking for work. And he wasn't Jewish. My father spoke a good Ukrainian language. He held his own. But the guy went for his rifle. It was on the other side of where we were standing. When my father saw this guy reach for his gun, he grabbed his one good leg and pulled the man off the horse. My father slammed him over the head with his boot and knocked him unconscious. Didn't touch the rifle. Didn't want to get involved with the weapon. But he kicked the horse and the horse ran off, so the amputee lost his transportation. The guy was out cold. We left him with his rifle and started running.

What amazed me about these trips out of the ghetto was the guts and strength my father had. The vision he had. Without a map or directions, he knew exactly where to go. We'd leave in the dark so the locals couldn't track us. We'd turn onto a potato field with no path, no landmarks. I used to whisper, "How do you know where you're going?" He'd head in a certain direction and we'd walk quietly for hours. Always in the fields, never on a main road. Somehow he would find the place he was looking for. Sometimes he'd ask where so-and-so lived. Very discreetly he'd make his way. He always had an answer for people when they asked, "How come you want to see this family?"

He'd say, "I'm here to do a job for them," or "They told me where they live and I'm lost."

About six weeks after Chayeleh and Froyem were killed, my

father connected with an acquaintance. A gentile. Through him, my father learned about a young Christian woman who passed away. She had documentation. Keep in mind that documentation from a gentile was a precious thing. At that time, no one traveled much and few people had passports. Well, my father met with his acquaintance and secured the passport. He planned to transform it into a passport for my oldest sister Ana. He had a photograph of Ana, about the right size. The young women were near the same age. Perhaps there was a few years of difference. Ana was seventeen, a striking girl with a round face and straight blonde hair. A beautiful, slender figure.

Leon's eldest sister, Ana Rubinstein, age 21, Russia, 1945.

In those days, the photograph on a passport was stamped with a wax seal. Using a knife from his tool bag, my father scraped off the wax. Carefully he peeled the photograph from the passport. He took my sister's photograph and cut it to the same size. I watched him work at this under primitive conditions. He didn't have his good tools because he lost his shop when we were forced into the ghetto. But he had his knife. And somehow he had the means of making a wooden duplicate of the stamp.

He spent a whole day working on the passport. Whatever wax he scraped away, he glued onto the picture. He kept scraping and gluing and he fixed up the passport so nobody could tell that it had been transformed. He used a flame to melt the wax stamp. He filled in the cracks. We kept on passing it to one another to see if anyone could pick up any flaws in this new arrangement. We couldn't find any. Once he finished the passport, he started talking to Ana. "You're the oldest. You have documentation now. There's nothing for you in Koretz. If we stay here together, we'll die together."

He convinced her to hit the road and go toward Russia. Toward Zhytomyr, which she knew. He had brought her there a few years earlier, to visit his sister. He told her to return to Zhytomyr and establish a new identity. The discussion took hours and hours. Plenty of tears. Wasn't an easy task. Taking a young woman who never left home and trying to convince her to leave on her own. God knows, he was persuasive. Finally, she agreed.

The next morning, my father snuck her out of the ghetto, like he did many times with me. He took her into the countryside and pointed in the direction of Russia. Gave her some confidence. Here was his first-born child, going with a little bag of food. A few slices of bread, maybe a bit of egg. That's all. He came back after she left and said, "At least she's out of the ghetto. She's out of Koretz. And hopefully, hopefully she's going to make it." He had tears in his eyes. We all did. We thought she'd be our only survivor.

Now there were six of us. My parents, me and my three sisters. Anyeh, Luba, and Batya, the baby. My father realized our chances for survival were better if we split up. He focused on finding a hiding place for me. Early one morning he took me to Richk, a nearby town. A friend of mine from school lived there. A gentile. He was a year or two older than me. My father thought maybe he'd take me in. Again, we were playing with fire because we weren't supposed to leave the ghetto. But we snuck out. Even though I knew this boy, I'd never been to his town. We walked and walked, through thick fields and running streams. Somehow my father found this boy's farm. We crept past their barn and approached the small farmhouse. Strange, I can't recall my friend's name. Must have blocked it out.

Hiding in Richk

My father knocked on the door of my friend's farmhouse in Richk. He introduced himself and asked to speak to the boy's father. But the father wasn't home. He was serving with the Russian army and the family didn't know where he was. My friend was the man of the house. He looked after his mother and two sisters. My father explained our situation to this boy and his mother. That I had nowhere to go and I could be killed. He talked the son into hiding me. My friend said, "Oh yes, I will. Of course, I will." The plan was that I'd live in the house, keep a low profile. Their farm wasn't near any neighbors. The closest place was a church and cemetery about three quarters of a mile away.

The boy's family called me Vasili, a Ukrainian name. Vasili became my new identity. Every day, I took the cow out to pasture and kept an eye on it. Most days, I just sat outdoors. That's how I earned my keep. Taking care of the cow used to be my friend's job. When I came back from the pasture, I ate dinner with the family and slept there at night. When the weather changed on the colder side, I stayed mostly in the house and the cow stayed in the barn. I did small chores. Cleaned the barn, fed the pigs and the horses. For six months, I stayed there. Nobody came to visit. Under the German occupation, there was no school for children, so there was little traffic. Everybody kept busy with chores.

My friend's mother had a brother who owned a nearby farm, about a mile away. I could see this brother's farm from their house. One Sunday, the woman's brother showed up after going to church. He saw me and asked, "Who is he?" The woman said, "This is Vasili. A friend of my son. He's staying with us for a while. His parents are sick." She gave him a story. By then, my accent was gone and I spoke a decent Ukrainian. My friend and his mother had worked with me on the language. Certain vowels I had to use. They made sure I pronounced every word the way they did. The brother, he asked me some questions. Then he came out and said, "This is a Jew."

The woman said, "No. That's not a Jew."

He said, "This is a Jew. I'm smart. I can tell these things."

Oh God, she really got angry at me. "Are you a Jew?" she asked.

I said, "No! Of course not!"

She took a frying pan and raised it in the air. She shouted, "Get out of my house! I don't harbor Jews!" She started screaming at me. Of course, it was a show. She knew who I was. I went along with it.

I said, "How dare you talk to me like this! I'm not a Jew. I'm a friend of your son."

She yelled, "Get out of my house!"

I ran out the door. To the cemetery near the church. You see, when she kicked me out of the house, she motioned the direction I should go. And hinted to the girls to keep an eye on me. Her son was not home at the time. But she made sure the girls knew exactly where I went. There was plenty of shrubbery at the cemetery. I sat in hiding behind some bushes. Listened to the birds chirping and insects crawling in the grass. Only one or two people visited the cemetery that day.

That night the woman came looking for me. She called out, "Vasili? Vasili?" And she brought me back to the house. Told me I could still stay with them but I had to go into hiding. She decided I should dig a hole in a corner of the barn where the cow stood. There was close to a foot of manure in that barn. They used it as fertilizer in the spring. I would live in a hole with a cover underneath the cow manure.

The son, my friend, still hadn't returned home. I kept asking, "Where is he?" His mother had no comment. Meanwhile, what was happening was her son had gone underground with the Banderites, Ukrainians fighting for their independence. My friend was spending most of his time in the forest, training to fight the Germans and the Russians. Anybody that was in the way. That's why my friend was never home.

Late that night, I dug my hole in the barn. Three feet by three feet by three feet. It was not lined, just dirt. The soil was very rich there. Kind of smelly because of the manure. The mother and I took some boards and laid them across the top of the hole. They weren't even nailed together. I knew I couldn't sit in a hole without air. Had to have something to breathe. There were no pipes available so I dug an opening that went outside the barn. Then I had access to air. Next, we had to make sure the cow wouldn't step in my corner. Those boards weren't strong enough to support the weight of the cow. The mother placed the cow's food on top of my hole. So most of the time, the cow's head would be there. If the cow turned around the other way, with her back to the wall, that'd be the end of me.

I lived in that hole, curled up like a worm, for almost two years. From twelve to fourteen years old. The woman of the house showed up once a day and shoveled out the manure to open up the hole. It was quite a bit of work for her. Then she gave me something to eat and drink. Nine out of ten times, it was a piece of bread and some milk. A lot of field mice and rats tried to get into my hole through the air vent. At night I'd be watching and trying to stop them from coming in. This was a warm spot for them, too. Who knows, they probably smelled the crumbs from my meal. I stayed in that hole most of the time. Occasionally I'd push hard to lift the cover up and crawl out to take a leak. Stretch my limbs. I went to the bathroom in that barn. It was my place for living. Many times I crawled out of the hole because of hunger pains. I knew the mother fed the pigs at a certain time each morning. I'd grab a potato from the pig's trough and eat on that for a while.

Most Sundays, the woman's brother would show up to the house. I could almost predict when he was coming. Sometimes in the daylight, I'd come out of the hole and look for him through the cracks in the barn. In those days, barns were made with vertical boards. There were no shingles, no outside layer. Just a structure with long boards. And the boards would shrink over time. So there would be a quarter of an inch space in between. Through the widest crack, I could see the field, the church, the cemetery. In that respect, I wasn't too smart, because anybody walking through the yard could see a shadow behind the crack, and they might figure out somebody was there.

After a month or two in the barn, my friend and his buddies from the underground began to appear. They'd have a get-together in the backyard between the farmhouse and the barn. They'd shoot off some guns, kick a ball around. I was always scared when I heard them with their guns, but my friend didn't reveal my hiding place. And after their little parties, they disappeared.

One night my father showed up. This was in the autumn of 1943. There was another slaughter that took place in Koretz and they murdered most of the Jews from the ghetto. My father and mother and three sisters took off the night before the killings. They went someplace in a field to hide but it wasn't secure. My father realized a field was no place to hide a family. Soon winter would come. He left my mother with the girls, went looking for hiding places. Came to see me. He knew he couldn't stay. But maybe my friend's mother could give some guidance where to go. He showed up in the middle of the night. She took him down to the barn. I came out of my hole and we embraced. I was shaking and crying, trying to explain why I was living in the hole. He held me tight, like he was never going to let go. Then he told me about the slaughter and how he was looking for another place to hide. Told me to stick it out. I might make it. He was worried about my sister Ana because there was no way of communicating with her. We talked for a while. Then he had to go back to my mother and sisters. We hugged again and he kissed me goodbye. He left in tears. Crying as much as I was. Even though he told me not to. Nothing I could do to help him. That was the last time I saw him.

Three or four days after my father's visit, my friend's mother came to the barn. She told me my father had been caught. He was being held in town and was going to be killed. She said, "I learned your father will be

executed today with some others they caught. They'll be taken to Kozak."
The forest where the mass graves were.

Keep in mind the local police knew my father. Knew he had a large family. After all, the police station was at the corner of Manasterskya Street. Before the war, the local police were among the people that bought bicycles and hope chests from my father. After the war broke out, a policeman came to see my father in the ghetto because he needed his bicycle repaired. My father got out his tools and fixed the man's bicycle. Fixed it for nothing. I was right there with my father. The policeman didn't give him a coin. Didn't even bring a slice of bread.

This policeman asked my father, "How did you make out in the first slaughter?"

My father told him, "I lost a son and a daughter."

The man replied, "That means you'll have more bread left for the rest of the family."

Was like a punch in the stomach to hear those words. My father handed the man his bicycle. And the policeman left.

When the police caught my father, my friend's mother told me they gave him a real beating. They knew my father had five children still alive. They wanted to know where the rest of the family was hiding. But my father, the way he was, he probably didn't even open his mouth. I hate to think what they did to him.

The day my father was executed, I was looking out a crack in the barn. Had a clear view of the road going from Koretz to Kozak. It was only half a mile away. I kept on looking and looking until finally I saw the horse-drawn wagon. Couldn't make out how many people were on the wagon, but I saw it heading toward the forest. The mass graves were already filled, so I presume they made my father dig his own grave. An hour went by and I began to hear the shots. One after the other, less than a minute apart. "Boom! Boom! Boom!" One of them was for my father. I felt so sick, I almost threw up. While I was crying, I started reciting *Kaddish*. Didn't have a prayer book but I said the first sentence. Kaddish for my father. Something I'll never forget.

A few days passed. I was sitting outside my hole, pressed against the crack in the wall. I saw a wagon, like the one that took my father into the forest. They were bringing more Jews to be executed at Kozak. As I was watching the wagon, one of the prisoners attacked the guard and jumped off. The guard was probably one of the local farmers with a rifle, volunteering to take Jews out to be shot. By that time, it was none of the Germans. It was the locals. In fact, the ones that killed my father were the locals.

I can see it clearly now, like it happened yesterday. This Jew kicked the local straight in the face. Grabbed his rifle, took the mechanism out and threw it away. He dropped the weapon, then jumped the wagon and took off running. Right next to the barn where I was hiding. He ran a quarter mile down the field. The local came into his own and assembled his rifle. Put some bullets in. These were single shot rifles, not automatics. The local kept on shooting. Each time the Jewish guy heard a shot, he would drop down, spread eagle on the field. The air was so thick, I could see the bullet moving over his head. Then the guy would pick himself up and start running again. The local would take another shot off. And I could see the bullet cutting through the air. Going at the right height. If that guy didn't fall, he'd be dead. I didn't know who he was. All I knew was he was taken out to be shot and he took a chance at running. And he got away. I said to myself, "Why couldn't that be my father?" But it wasn't meant to be. My father couldn't get away.

Soon after my father was killed, my mother showed up at the barn with my sisters Anyeh, Luba and Batya. The woman of the house came and took me out of the hole. She kept saying, "Say hello and goodbye. They can't stay here. People will find out. They have to leave." It was a short reunion, maybe fifteen minutes. My mother told me she didn't know what to do. Where to hide. How to get food. I was beside myself with tears. She told me not to leave, because if anyone could survive, it could be me. My sisters and mother were rail thin. Wearing ragged, dirty clothes. Anyeh was sixteen years old, Luba was six, Batya was four. I hugged them tight and felt their long hair against my face. Then my friend's mother shooed them out of the barn.

I'm not exactly sure what happened next, but I assume my mother and sisters were rounded up in Richk by local farmers. Maybe even the woman's brother was involved. They were probably taken out to the same forest where my father and Froyem and Chayeleh were murdered. I don't know if they made them dig their own graves. I was in the hole in the barn when they were killed. There was nothing I could do. Just curl up in my hole. Disappear in my tears.

Five months after my mother and sisters were killed, my friend's mother came to the barn. She told me I couldn't stay there anymore. I had to move outside to the potato field. She was much concerned with her son in the underground. Didn't want me near the house. It was March 1944. Springtime. The potatoes were just starting to grow. We went out at night and she handed me a shovel. We walked to the potato field, a few hundred yards from the barn. The dirt was moist and heavy and the sky was dark. I took out some roots and dug the hole. Felt like I was digging my grave. The hole was about the same size as the one in the barn. I used a few boards to cover it. On top of the boards were potato plants. Here again, nothing was nailed together. There was a small opening in the top for me to breathe.

The woman looked at the hole when I was done. She was critical. What was I going to do with the dirt? She didn't want a pile of dirt. That looked suspicious. She wanted everything taken away, clean. I scattered the dirt the best I could, then I folded myself up in the hole and pulled the cover over my head. I sat there. Didn't know if she would bring me food. The potatoes weren't grown yet. If they were, I would have eaten them raw.

I stayed in that hole in the field for two months. The woman showed up each night and dropped off a bit of food. Some bread or a leftover from supper. For liquid she gave me milk from the cow or water. There were a lot of mice scampering around the field, looking for food. They crawled over me like I was a potato root. I was full of fear, not knowing if I would be discovered, not knowing what could happen at any time. I never knew if I was going to turn into target practice for my friend or his buddies in the underground. I tried to fill my mind with thoughts about my family before the war. About our house on Manasterskya Street. About my grandparents and cousins. About going to shul. Somehow, I managed.

Discovered by the Red Army

By May of 1944, I was fourteen years old, still living in the potato field. I didn't realize the Russians had liberated the area a few months before. The woman never told me. There I was, smelly and filthy. Never washed my body, never brushed my teeth. Hadn't had a haircut in years. Wearing the same pants and shirt from when my father brought me to Richk. By now, those clothes were rags. I'd been alone all that time. Didn't know the war was coming to an end.

Early one morning, around three o'clock, I heard a lot of activity outside my hole. People were there. And the language I heard wasn't German. It was Russian. A whole company of Russian soldiers was combing the potato field. There might have been two hundred and fifty of them. The Russians had mounted a campaign against the Ukrainian underground, the Banderites. They were searching for my friend because he was quite a leader. They advanced across the field, pounding the ground with bayonets. Sixteen inches long. Soon they hit the board covering the hole I was in. I heard the bayonet going through the wood. I was far enough from it so it didn't touch me. The board was six or eight inches below the surface. Just deep enough to hold up a potato plant. It was like they put a pitchfork into the hole and lifted up the cover. I was exposed in the moonlight. All folded up and shivering.

Right away the soldiers who found me summoned their captain. They pointed at me, spit on the ground. They started talking to me in Russian. I saw the red star of the Russian uniform and couldn't say a word. I didn't know what to make of it. They motioned me to come out, but I was too shaken to move. So they pulled me out by my neck. They dragged me to my friend's farmhouse and put me down outside. They kept talking to me but I couldn't speak. It was freezing cold in the middle of the night and I was chilled to the bone.

When the sun came up, a woman captain approached me. She was in her forties. This captain realized I wasn't the guy they were looking for. Something wasn't right. She started talking to me in Yiddish. Asked me if I was Jewish. Told me she was Jewish, too. I just sat there, numb. Didn't realize what was taking place. She said, "This is not the man we want. This is somebody we have to take care of." Soon someone put a blanket on me. Gave me some bread and water. Once the woman captain came, they treated me like a different person.

They put me on a wagon and brought me to a nearby barn. Handed me a pail of water to wash up. Gave me a Russian uniform. It was two or three sizes too big, but warm. And they gave me a bit more food. Still I couldn't speak. The Jewish captain appeared. She realized the family had been hiding me. She told me, "These are bad people." She didn't know how I survived. She told me she was looking for the son, my friend.

The Russians found my friend in the cemetery later that morning and killed him. They took the mother and daughters out of the house and burned it down. Burned the farm, too. But they didn't harm the mother and daughters. I told the captain that the family was good to me. Without them, I couldn't have survived. This woman captain was the one who told me the Russians had been in the area close to six months while I was in the potato field. She couldn't understand why I was still in hiding. She said maybe they were using me for a bargaining chip. If something happened, they could say, "By the way, I have a Jew. I'll trade him for this and that." She told me I was lucky to have survived.

Another captain was called in. A young guy, twenty-six years old. He took me under his wing, made sure I stayed with his group. He gave me an automatic weapon and a military hat. And so I became a little soldier with the Red Army. My captain brought me to Koretz to find people I might recognize. Some of the surviving Jews had returned, trying to piece their lives together. I saw a few neighbors. They were living in whatever house was available. The captain asked, "Where is your house?" I pointed to the area where my house used to be and it was gone. Must have been burned down. Nothing to hold onto.

Before the first slaughter in Koretz, I woke up one night and heard some noise in our backyard. I looked out the window and saw my father digging a hole. At his side I saw documents, probably birth certificates and the deed to the house, and he might have had some silver and my mother's ring. He buried all of these items. I watched him from the window until he filled in the hole with dirt. He washed his hands at the water barrel and returned to the house. I went back to sleep. Never brought it up with my father. When I returned to Koretz with the Russian captain, I told him about the buried goods. But since my house was gone, I didn't know where to search. The house left no footprint. It was completely erased. Just land. Nothing to prove I ever lived there.

The captain took me every other day to Koretz to see new people. At night I stayed with the Russians. They gave me a military cot to sleep in, the kind of cot the United States Army is still using today. And they shared their food with me. Canned sardines, canned cheese, and dried potatoes. There was plenty for me to eat. The food was made in the United States, except for the potatoes. I could see the labels on the cans, even though I couldn't read them. The potatoes probably came from Russia. Eating that food was a way I regained my strength.

The Russian soldiers' main job was going on missions to hunt down and kill local Ukrainians who were fighting for their independence. I went on these missions with the Russians. They were absolutely ruthless. They'd walk into a house and break the door down. Most of the time, they'd find women and children. Without asking questions, they'd start shooting. They didn't want to take any fire from the locals. I had just come out of hell. And then to see this hell being given to the Ukrainians. Was too much. Even though most of them treated the Jews like dogs, I didn't feel so hostile to the locals at that time. It was the locals that murdered my family, but they also saved my life. To see such violence against them was unacceptable to me. But I had nowhere else to go.

After they finished their missions in Koretz, I traveled with the Russians to Rovno. They took over a barracks, a jail and a police station. I moved in there with them. From that base they began launching attacks. They wanted to scare the locals into another way of life, scare them into thinking that fighting the Russian government was never going to work.

One afternoon, they gathered twenty-five or thirty young men. The youngest one was twelve and the oldest was twenty-five. They set up a lynching spot in the marketplace. It was a big open space and the lynching platform was huge. It was going the length of a football field. I saw soldiers building this thing out of logs. I didn't understand what they were constructing, but I knew something dramatic was going to happen. It took a day to build.

The next morning, they brought six truckloads of these young guys. And they hung them all. I couldn't believe what was happening. The trucks would pull up to a section of the platform and they'd put up four guys at a time. The truck would back up and deliver another group. They put up four more and four more. They had soldiers guarding the area so nobody would raise any hell. I was one of the soldiers guarding the platform. Other soldiers dragged in the locals to watch the mass hangings. Before it was done, I saw twenty-five of these guys hanging there. There was no trial. Nothing. It was a horrible scene. Some of them were peeing. Some were going in their pants. I was standing in front of the lynching area, like the rest of the guards. Felt dizzy and sick. I said to myself, "I can't take this." God forbid someone would try to run and I would have to start shooting. When this mass hanging happened, it turned me all the way around. I knew my days with the Russians were coming to an end.

Around that time, I used to walk the streets in Rovno by myself, getting familiar with my surroundings. I wore my Russian uniform and carried my gun. It was the first time I'd been in a metropolitan city.

The population of Rovno was four times the size of Koretz. The homes were more sophisticated, the buildings were taller. Instead of two-story buildings, they had four stories, with high ceilings and high doors. The streets were wider, there were dirt sidewalks. Koretz didn't have any of that.

While I was walking one day, a boy my age came over and started talking to me in Russian. He asked if I was Jewish and we struck up a conversation. I learned he was a Jewish orphan. Like me, his parents and family had been killed in the war. He had survived by hiding in a forest, where he lost a toe to frostbite. His name was Aharon Golub.

Aharon was living in the city with his uncle, Usher Edelman. Usher had two sons and a wife that had somehow survived the war. The five of them occupied a house. Aharon took a liking to me and brought me to his uncle's place. At first, Aharon's relatives didn't know what to make of me, with my Russian uniform and gun. But we got to talking and I told them I came from Koretz. They knew some people that knew my family. Pretty soon, Aharon's aunt made a soup of herring and potatoes. Salt was hard to get. It was at a premium. When she was making the soup, she said, "We'll have to live with salt from the herring." The warm smell of the herring filled the house. When the soup was done, she served me a hot bowl with my own spoon. It was the most delicious thing I'd tasted in years.

While I was eating, Aharon's aunt and uncle told me they had connections with the shul in Rovno, and that the shul had received care packages from the United States. Stuff sent by Jewish organizations. Clothing and shoes and other goods. Maybe I ought to avail myself of some of the items. But I said, "I'm happy with what I have." Even though all I had to wear was the Russian uniform. Then I left their place.

I was with the Russians for another week. We went on missions in a little town, not far from Rovno. Early in the morning we would strike. The missions would start at three o'clock and they'd be finished by six or seven a.m. My captain, the guy that was my mentor, he was killed one morning. He went on a mission and walked into a house. I'm sure he had his gun drawn but was hit first. The man in the house probably had a couple of guns and opened fire.

When my mentor was killed, my stay with the Russians was definitely over. I didn't want to be with them. While my mentor was alive, he talked about sending me to school in Russia. A military school. He had some connections. I never really wanted to do that, but it showed he cared. I don't remember my mentor's name, but we were close. He took me everyplace. He and I would leave at night. He would go and find a woman to have sex with. And I would be watching. Sitting there, I watched him rape dozens of local women. It was brutal. And he wasn't the only one. I saw other soldiers doing the same thing. Raping women was the soldiers' way of relieving themselves. Many of these men had wives at home they were far away from. The day after the rapes, I would see these same soldiers crying, thinking about their wives and children. How much they missed them.

Right before I left the army, the commander of my unit asked me to take care of his horse. A beautiful stallion. This commander was always on the stallion, riding bareback. Me, I was never on top of a horse. But I agreed to look after it. Mostly I wanted to see what riding was like. So I brought the horse to an open field and jumped on. Well, that horse started galloping. Mind you, he wasn't familiar with me. He was running furiously and I could barely hold on. All of a sudden, the horse stopped and I went flying. I didn't actually go that far, but it felt like I was flying a hundred meters. When I crashed, I thought I was going to be killed. I don't know how I landed without breaking any bones. And I was lucky the horse didn't break a hoof from all the rat holes in the field. I was beaten up from such a bad fall. Picked myself up and limped back to the horse. He just stayed there, waiting for me. I brought the horse back to the commander.

I told him, "I took a gallop on the horse and he dropped me."

The commander said, "If he doesn't know you, he won't trust you."

After my incident with the horse, I was so sore I could barely move my arms and legs. I went back to Aharon's uncle's house and asked, "Can I help myself to some clothing through the shul? I'm trying to leave the unit because things aren't working out." After all, I wasn't going to walk around with a Russian uniform anymore. They took me to the shul and I picked up a shirt and pants and some boots, about three or four sizes bigger than what I needed. Took off the Russian uniform and went back to the unit. Didn't want them to think I left without permission. I told them my mentor was dead and things were not what I wanted to pursue. I was going out on my own. They said, "Okay, you can go." There were no papers to sign. I wasn't there officially. I was there by invitation. They told me, "If you ever run into trouble, you can come back."

Novograd Volynsk

Once I left the Russians, there was no reason for me to stay in Rovno. It was July 1944. I decided to go to Novograd Volynsk, a town ten or fifteen miles outside of Koretz. I had heard through some survivors that I had distant relatives there. Some cousins on my father's side. Novograd Volynsk was a small town, maybe half a dozen streets. I knew the family name, so it couldn't be too hard to find these people. I showed up at their house one night and mentioned my family name. The woman of the house was skeptical because I had no proof of the relationship. But she took me in. Gave me room and board. The house had only two bedrooms, so I slept on the dirt floor. It was a woman in her fifties, her daughter, son-in-law and grandson.

The son-in-law was a member of the communist party and worked for the Russian government. He was in charge of a photographic lab. Gave me some work in the back of the photo studio, touching up features on the negatives. The negatives were made of glass plates with a silver coating. I worked there for a month. The other job the son-in-law had was overseeing Russian propaganda films. They were shown to the Russian army and to peasants in surrounding towns. These films promoted the philosophy of the Russians. I'm talking about collective farms, working in factories, building the means to support the Red Army. The films were transported from town to town and shown at night in open fields. Two or three dozen people would show up. All for free. While I was in Novograd Volynsk, I showed half a dozen films. My job was to put the reel on the projector.

After four weeks, I left the family. I saw no future with them. They were cold to me and I didn't feel welcome. We had no history together, no real connection. I decided to go back to Koretz, where I was familiar. Walked part of the way and hitchhiked. In Koretz, I found some discarded wood and built myself a little box. For a while, I stood on a corner and shined shoes. Wasn't a steady job. Nobody had much money. During that time, I stayed with neighbors. With children of neighbors. With acquaintances, Jewish families. It was a tough life to keep my head above water. After a few weeks, I outstayed my welcome with these families. I couldn't ask for another meal. It was hard enough for them to provide for their own.

When I was trying to figure out what to do next, I was recruited by a guy in Koretz dealing in the black market. Cigarettes, salt, sugar and yeast. There was quite a demand for these goods. Most of the stuff came from who knows where. I recognized a few of the kids working for this dealer from my school days. For them it was a way to make a little money and get a meal. The dealer made sure I learned the ropes before I started peddling. For four or five days, I observed the technique of the kids and that's how I was trained. They would pick someone dressed in decent clothes and walk alongside him, saying, "If you're interested, I'm selling yeast and salt at a good price."

It was a risky situation. The Russians were against business, especially a black market business. For us kids, it wasn't that complicated because the dealer kept most of the profits. The dealers recruited children because the Russians would be more lenient on us. The grown-ups would definitely find themselves being executed. But the worst thing that would happen to us kids would be getting sent to Siberia to work in a coal mine.

I got friendly with one of the peddlers. He was an orphan like me but his father's house was still intact. In one bedroom lived a young woman with her daughter. This woman used to know my friend's father. She was about thirty years old and her daughter was five or six. My friend stayed in the other bedroom. Well, I needed a roof over my head. This kid told me I could share his bed. Barely two people fit in there. But we were young. We made it work. I stayed there a few nights with them, less than a week. There was a Russian soldier who used to break in and have sex with the woman. There were hardly any doors between us. She would be sleeping with her daughter and the guy would crawl into their bed. She would try to fight him off by putting the daughter in between her and the soldier. I was in bed with my friend, pretending to sleep. The rapes from the soldier went on every night. After a few days, I couldn't take it. So I moved out from that house.

Once I was trained on the black market, the dealer sent me to Novograd Volynsk to peddle cigarettes and salt. I knew the town since I'd lived there for a month. I tried to hitchhike but couldn't get a lift, so I walked most of the distance and carried my bundle. It consisted of ten packs of cigarettes and two pounds of salt, maybe three pounds of salt. Divided into little packages. I was supposed to get so much per package and so much per cigarette. Some cigarettes were sold as singles because most people couldn't afford a whole pack. I left Koretz around noontime. By the time I got to Novograd Volynsk, the sun was going down. I didn't know where I was going to spend the night, but I could always sleep on a bench in a park. As soon as I came into the town, though, I got picked up by the police. It was like they were waiting for me. Hadn't even made a trade.

When I was picked up, they realized I was one of the kids working the black market. They took away my goods and asked who was the dealer.

I said, "I don't know him." They put me in a lockup. Wasn't much of a jail, just a wooden building. They said they'd talk to me in the morning. At least I had some shelter for the night. The police were more interested in the salt and cigarettes than in me. After they confiscated the goods, they kept it for their own needs. They themselves were probably trading it. That's the way the system worked.

In the morning, I knocked on the jail door and said I needed to use the outhouse in the yard. It was a simple structure made of vertical boards. The guard took me there and walked back to the jail, keeping an eye on me. I relieved myself quickly and looked out the widest crack. The back of the outhouse led to a street. From my days in hiding, I was used to these things. The boards were flimsy, just nailed on. One board might have been eight or ten inches wide. And believe me, I was skinny. I popped a board and took off toward the street. The guard was still up front keeping an eye on the outhouse door. But I was gone. I ran all the way back to Koretz. Must have made it in record time.

To the Orphanage

Back in Koretz, the first thing I did was find the black market dealer. Told him what happened in Novograd Volynsk. That I was caught but didn't squeal. He accepted my story. These things happened all the time. He asked if I wanted another assignment. I told him, "No." I didn't want to stay in Koretz anymore. There was nothing left for me there. I decided to go back to Rovno, where I remembered the tasty herring soup that Aharon's aunt made. So I worked my way to Rovno.

My first day there, I bumped into Israel Fuchs, a blacksmith from Manasterskya Street. He grabbed my arm. You know, I looked like my father. He started hugging and kissing me. Wouldn't let go. Israel lost his wife and children in the war and remarried another woman from Koretz. He'd taken over a Jewish house in Rovno and was living there with his wife, his new child, the wife's father, and some other survivors.

Israel took me in and I stayed with them a few months. Israel's father-in-law had previously owned a factory that manufactured socks. When the war broke out, he stashed away a major piece of equipment. After the war, he managed to bring the machine from its hiding place to the house in Rovno. It occupied quite a bit of space. Israel's father-in-law didn't know how to operate it. The guy was a businessman, not a worker. Most equipment in those days, even though automated, was operated by human power. A person had to turn a wheel or peddle with his feet. Like a sewing machine. The father-in-law spent days and days trying to get his machine to work. At that time there was no livelihood for people, no way to go out and make a living. And this equipment just sat and sat. Being mechanically minded, I tried to help him get it started. I was intrigued. Here was a piece of equipment that actually produced socks. Until then, I thought socks were handmade, like mittens were knitted. Every day for a week we tried to get it to work. He would tell me what he'd seen the machine do. But we had no success. Couldn't get it going.

Meanwhile, Israel's house was a place where people showed up looking for relatives. Looking for loved ones. Everyone was searching for someone. One day a guy showed up from Russia looking for his daughter. He knew his wife was dead, but like many people, he was holding out hope that his daughter was still living. Soon it became apparent that his daughter had been killed. He was devastated. Sat at the table with his head in his hands. Every now and then a sob came from his mouth.

Israel and his father-in-law knew this fellow had left Russia with papers for himself and his daughter. That meant he had the means. They helped the man grieve for his daughter and then convinced him that I could be his child. That he should take me with him. I had no family, no roots in Rovno. I wanted to go toward England, maybe the United States. Someplace where the Russians were not in control. Then maybe I'd be able to work my way out. England was the number one destination talked about for young people. The United States. Canada was a destination. But without papers, I couldn't leave Rovno. Sure enough, this guy agreed to take me. He couldn't save his own child but he could save someone else's.

He took me with him, heading toward Czechoslovakia. That was his first destination. We boarded a train in Rovno and eventually it arrived in the city of Bytom, in Southern Poland. It was a slow trip because we had to sit and wait for military trains to pass by. We arrived after midnight. He asked for directions to his relatives and we got to their place in the middle of the night. They, too, had moved into a Jewish house. We knocked on the door. Of course, they didn't dare open the door for us and we stayed all night in the hallway. In the morning, they realized who he was and let us in. His relatives saw I was an orphan. They weren't interested in me sticking around. After all, they'd have to feed me, they'd have to take care of me. They said the best thing was for me to join the orphanage in Bytom. So we had a bite in the house and then they dropped me off at the orphanage.

It was a good place to stay, that orphanage house. I was off the street. Had a roof and a couple of meals a day. They had electricity. The means to clean up and wash. A Jewish relief agency ran the orphanage with money from the United States. There must have been two dozen boys and girls at the orphanage, all of them Jewish. Everybody kept to themselves. No one talked about what they went through. I made friends with a boy named Kalman Offir, who was a few years older and larger in size. All he had to do was stand next to me and I felt secure. A few days later, Aharon Golub showed up. A great feeling to see him again. By now it was the end of May 1945, a few weeks after the war ended. I was fifteen years old.

I stayed at the orphanage for three months, until my buddies and I were recruited by a Zionist group. These organizations showed up at the orphanage to find teenagers and bring them to *Eretz Yisrael*, the Land of Israel. Israel at that time was British Palestine.

Each organization had its own political agenda. They talked to us calmly and tried to convince us they were the best choice. Shom Eretz Hayer was conservative. Dror was more of a socialist organization. Some of them were part of the *Irgun*, the underground organization resisting the British in Palestine. Each one promised us the world. The Zionist idea was to get hold of kids they could mold to their way of thinking. In a quiet way.

Kalman, Aharon and I decided to stick with the group called Dror. There was really no reason, just a decision that a couple of kids made. The organization's main aim was to get us to Palestine. At that time, the country didn't allow any Jews in. The guys from Dror didn't know how or when they would get us in, but that was their plan. Maybe it would happen that year, maybe the next year. Well, we were going no place. So we stuck it out at the orphanage.

Displaced Persons Camp

In August of 1945, the guys from Dror came to get us. It was a hot, sunny afternoon. The plan was to take a train from Bytom, Poland, across the border into Germany. There we'd enter a displaced persons camp in Leipheim. How were we going to do it? We had no papers, no money. But the guys from Dror said they'd get us on the train and keep an eye on us. We were told, "Two can stay in this car. Two can stay in that car." They broke us up, so there wasn't a big group of kids. Those cars were crowded. Some of us wound up alone on the floor. It took a day and a half or two days to get to Leipheim. We had no

Leon Rubinstein, age 15, displaced persons camp, Leipheim, Germany, 1945.

food and I was by myself in a corner. Didn't get to see Kalman or any of my buddies from the orphanage. We went through cities and towns but we weren't allowed to get off the train. Then, sure enough, we got to Leipheim.

Leipheim was occupied by Americans. American trucks and troops were everywhere. It was the first time I was exposed to black soldiers. The American army was segregated at that time. Those soldiers were like cowboys, speeding the streets in big, heavy duty trucks. Making corners at 50 miles per hour. Driving in the middle of the road with disregard for life. The trucks were ready to tip over. People were running away from them. To me, it was a new world. To see these guys, total black, driving like maniacs in these huge vehicles.

The guys from Dror brought us to the displaced persons camp, a holding station for refugees. It had been a German military camp and was well equipped. They had electricity and running water, even toilets, something we hadn't seen before. It was a long, straight barrack with American folding cots. In the orphanage, we'd slept on mattresses stuffed with straw, the type of bed I was accustomed to. But in the barrack, we each had our own cot and a military issue blanket. When we arrived, the staff at the camp sprayed us for lice. Then they showed us boxes of used clothes that had been shipped from the United States. Some of us had been wearing the same clothes since the war began. We picked out clean shirts and pants.

There were probably a thousand refugees living at the camp. My barrack was full of orphans like me that came from all over. I met a boy named Ezra Sherman and we became fast friends. In my group, there were thirty-two of us, all teenagers. Kalman was the oldest one at seventeen. We had a guidance counselor named Hannah, a petite young woman from Poland. She was picked to be a leader. Hannah had a younger brother, Shlomo, who was also with our group. Then there was Yasha Steinberg, a man in his thirties who gave us additional guidance. He was low-key, not dictating. Didn't try to be a parent figure.

Aside from the clothes on our backs, none of us had possessions. No suitcases. Nothing to carry. Didn't have a comb or a toothbrush or even a razor. Some boys in our group were shaving already. If there was a razor in the barracks, the boys all shared. A bunch of kids had trouble with their teeth. Keep in mind we hadn't brushed our teeth in years. For a rotting tooth, we'd take a shoelace and yank the tooth right out. Came out with a hunk of meat on it, bleeding forever. The kid would be screaming his head off.

Aside from toothaches, few of us had medical problems. We were undernourished but resilient. I complained about my back, about aches and pains I had. Hannah, the guidance counselor, gave me the means to go to a medical clinic where I was examined by a German doctor. This doctor told me I had rheumatoid arthritis from being buried so long in a damp environment. I heard his German accent and didn't trust him. Not one bit. I took the trolley to the clinic a few times. The first time I went with somebody from Dror. Next time I went on my own. I got therapy once or twice but there was nothing much they could do for me.

In general, the girls had a tougher time than the boys because of their hygiene. Some of them were getting their period and there were no sanitation devices. We were aware of that. After all, we were sharing the same room. There was hardly any privacy. We didn't take many showers. There was no soap, no shampoo. Just used a faucet to wash our faces. If we wanted to wash our hair, we wet it down with water.

The food we ate was mainly canned goods from the United States. Cheese in a can, sardines. Crackers in packages. We ate a lot of those. Bread was not readily available and when we got it, it was stale. We never got a glass of milk. No fresh produce. We were always fighting for sweet things, like jam. Everybody wanted it. We craved sugar. A few adults had tiny, folding can openers. Just a little hook to catch onto the lid. They opened the can by moving the hook back and forth. Many people cut their hands. A lot of kids had black and blue marks on their fingers. But we did what was necessary to eat.

The camp was financed by a Jewish relief agency but the different groups within the camp were controlled by the Zionist underground. They were the ones giving orders, making decisions. We saw them occasionally, but they were mostly invisible. They spent their time traveling back and forth to Eastern Europe and Russia, finding orphans and bringing them across the border. The underground was spread out and had hundreds of people searching for recruits. Meanwhile, the organizations at the camp worked each other's territories and tried to convince the refugees to switch over. They had better facilities, a better way of life, a better philosophy. That sort of thing. We stayed with Dror, even though we never signed any papers. It was a verbal commitment we made.

The days went by with a little learning of Hebrew. The guys from Dror kept it low pressure. They tried to boost morale, have a group mentality. We sang songs, got acquainted with one another. It was a subdued atmosphere. No rowdiness among the kids. Everybody had their story but were keeping it to themselves. I was quiet, very lonely. I tried to learn from people I bumped into. Maybe they heard about somebody I knew. My relatives, my friends. I knew my sister Ana was alive because someone had seen her in Koretz right after the war. But I didn't know where she was or how to contact her. I tried to talk to people that might know something. Maybe they heard of my relatives in Russia. Anything.

In other barracks, I connected with survivors from Koretz. A boy named Eli Gluzband was there with his sister and father. Our fathers had been friends back home. Moshe Troskovski also came from our town. He was there with a sister. Maybe they knew how people were killed or how they survived. People talked about living in the forests, foraging for food. I learned a lot just from listening. Moshe Troskovski had an important friend in that camp, a leader in the Warsaw ghetto. Everyone looked up to him. Whenever I had a chance, I'd run to their barrack. Sit down and have a chat. The refugees created their own little corners. Some were more organized than others. Most of the adults at the camp stayed a short time, on their way to Canada, to England, to Argentina. They fended for themselves. The groups of orphans stayed longer. My group stayed for eight months, from August 1945 to April 1946. We had a lot of time on our hands.

The camp provided entertainment to help us feel better about what we had gone through. Yehudi Menuhin, the Jewish violin player, he came from the United States to give a little joy. It was the first time in my life I went to a concert. The grown-ups sat on chairs and the kids sat on the floor. Menuhin played such beautiful music but it was haunting at the same time. Eery sounds that cut me on the inside. The famous pianist Arthur Rubinstein was also supposed to perform, but he never showed up. From time to time, there were plays put on by the different groups in the camp. And there were parades. We were taught how to march in an orderly manner. My first picture was taken when I was part of those parades. A black and white photograph. I was fifteen and a half years old.

My group didn't stray far from the camp. We were told not to walk on the field because of ordinance that was left over from the German military. There was a small airport attached to the camp. Wasn't being used. Again, we were cautioned not to walk off the main drag. We didn't

go into Leipheim regularly, but we wandered in there a few times. Didn't have money, even if there was anything to be bought. There were few German men in the streets. Most of them were dead. But there were a lot of German women. In fact, women drove the trolleys. We were there just a few months after Leipheim was bombed. Houses were in rubble. I saw rooms open to the sky, furniture knocked on its side. But the town came back fast. The railroad station was in fairly good shape. The sidewalks were

Leon's friend, Kalman Offir and Leon Rubinstein carrying flags, displaced persons camp, Leipheim, Germany, 1945.

84

walkable and broken glass was getting cleaned up. It was remarkable the way that town came back to life.

The whole time we were at the camp, the underground was silently working on a way to get us into British Palestine. We knew our destination but nobody talked about it. There were rumors here and there. We asked questions of our leaders, but they wouldn't offer any information. Even if they knew, they wouldn't say. Once we realized we were going to be moving out of the camp, even the destination in Palestine was kept secret. Mine was the first group picked to sail to Palestine. There might have been other groups on our boat, but we were separated. Nobody intertwined. We were on our own.

II. Teenage Years in Palestine, 1946-1950

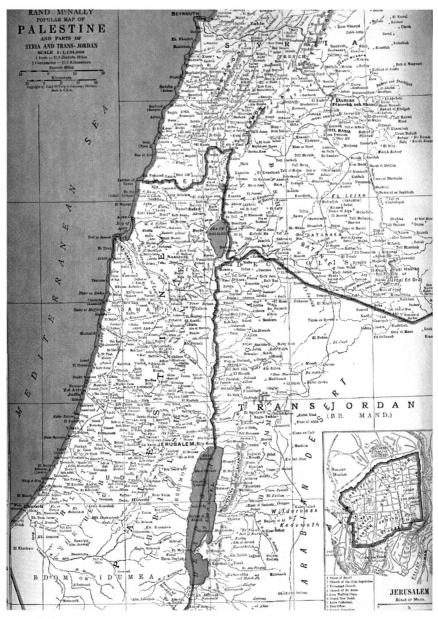

Map of Palestine, 1938
© Rand McNally, reproduced with permission R.L.08-S-63

Smuggled into Palestine

We left the displaced persons camp in Leipheim in springtime, April of 1946. It was quite a job to take thirty-two kids without documentation and provide them with papers. But the leaders from Dror handled it. They got fake documentation showing we were Greek refugees returning home. They gave us Greek names so no one would suspect we were Slavic Jews heading to Palestine. Before we boarded the train in Leipheim, the guys from Dror told us, "Don't make a big deal. Stay low." In this manner, we crossed the border from Germany into France. Checking papers was done on the hush and hush. The guys from Dror must have been paying people off. It went quickly and none of us were held back.

In a day or two, we got to Marseille and were rushed into the port at night. A couple of guys from the *Palmach* met us there. The Palmach was the striking force of the *Haganah*, the Jewish paramilitary in British Palestine. They led us to an enormous ship called the Champollion, but they didn't board with us. There were other people aboard that oversaw the situation. Us kids were dispersed. A couple went here, a couple went there. We were each assigned a hammock hanging below deck. Another kid was paired with me, but we didn't stick together. I didn't see Kalman or Aharon or any of my friends the whole time I was aboard. Didn't know who was protecting me. The conditions on the ship were primitive. I can't even describe a bathroom. Don't remember how we relieved ourselves. There was no shower, no sink. We ate little on that trip. Someone would show up and pass out a piece of bread, a drink of water. Sometimes I felt I wouldn't make it. Many times on that trip, I looked out the side of the ship. Wondering what was down there in the Mediterranean. I saw dolphins in the water, jumping and swimming.

It was a five-day trip and we were supposed to stay below deck. But after the second or third day, I wandered. Just to get myself familiar. After all, I was curious. Was never on a ship before. And it was a huge vessel. Each time I wandered off, a big man would come over and say, "Go back." I didn't know who this man was and he terrified me. He carried a little bag on his back. Whenever I explored, he was right there. I couldn't tell what language he spoke. Maybe Greek or Turkish. Or Arabic. When I laid in the hammock, I kept looking to see if he was nearby. One morning I was exploring the front of the boat. I saw the anchors and chains and the hole where the anchor slid down. The rings on the chain were heavy and powerful. I kept touching them. This guy was right behind me. I thought to myself, "What if he pushes me down the anchor hole?"

The ship stopped at different ports. Some people were aboard for shorter rides. We stopped in Morocco, then in Alexandria, Egypt. At that time, Egypt was run by the British government. We didn't get off the ship, but we saw British authorities for the first time. We stayed at Alexandria for half a day. And then we were off the coast of Palestine. Our destination was Haifa. Everyone was getting excited. Until then, we didn't know if we were really going to get there. As we came into the port of Haifa, I saw two gigantic stacks, which were power plants. "What could that be?" I wondered. I'd never seen anything of that magnitude. Then I saw the majestic landscape of Mount Carmel. Houses built into the sides of rolling green hills. The bright sun overhead. And to the right, the port city of Haifa. It was April 26, 1946. We had arrived.

The British didn't provide clearance to bring us into the country. But because we were kids, they weren't going to push us. When we disembarked, I saw all the orphans from the displaced persons camp in Leipheim. I hadn't seen them all trip long and here they were, climbing down the ladder one after another. So relieved to see my friends. The British fumigated us right there in the open. They sprayed our heads, our clothes, our bodies. And that stuff stuck to us. I think it was DDT. It killed lice, mites, anything we carried.

We were loaded onto a military bus. The British were yelling at us so we didn't talk much. They wanted to make sure we followed orders. We were hauled to a British military base outside of Haifa called Atlit. It was surrounded by a chain link fence with barbed wire on top. Here again, they put us in one barrack. The girls and boys together. In the barrack, we felt the heat. Even though it wasn't summer, it was warm. The conditions at this camp were a little better than in Leipheim. There were outside showers, partially enclosed. The boys took showers first, then the girls went. There was no hot water but we didn't care. We had a little soap. It was the first wash in I don't know how long.

The British brought us dairy products. Little jars of plain yogurt. In Hebrew they called it *lebania*. And we had fruit. Vegetables for breakfast, cucumbers and tomatoes. Physically we started to feel better, because the food was more nutritious. We slept on little cots, with a blanket to cover ourselves. No sheets. We stayed in our barrack all day long. Weren't allowed to roam and explore. But morale wasn't too bad. We questioned each other, "How long are we going to stay?" We could see the barbed wire fence not far from the barracks. None of us were going to climb that fence.

After ten days, word got around that we would be out of there. One night we were awakened, just after midnight. The door popped open. And we quickly snuck out. In silence we walked to the fence that surrounded the barracks. There was a big hole in it, wide enough for us to climb through. I saw two guys holding each side of the fence, protecting the wires so nobody would get cut. It was pitch dark. We were rushed through the hole in the fence and then the guys divided us into small groups. Five kids with one leader. We hiked all the way up Mount Carmel.

We came to wide, open fields north of Zikhron Ya'akov, a Jewish populated town well-known for producing wine. We stayed in the fields. We didn't see any activity, nobody looking for us. We stayed low, resting on blankets, protecting ourselves from the outside environment. The leaders gave us some food. Once it got dark, we were broken up into small groups again. We walked down the other side of the mountain on a narrow path. It was a total of twenty miles. We walked all the way to Kibbutz Yagur.

Leon Rubinstein, age 17,
Kibbutz Yagur, Palestine, 1947.

Kibbutz Yagur

We got to the kibbutz in the morning and the leaders made us take showers outside. No hot water, but each of us got a piece of soap. Each of us also got a toothbrush and a small tube of toothpaste. "They're yours," they told us, "hold onto them." They distributed a set of new clothes. Short khaki pants, a khaki shirt with short sleeves, and an undershirt. Underwear, they gave us. And a hat with a flap, to protect our necks from the sun. The girls got little dresses. Everybody got sandals.

They called me Eliezer, the Hebrew form of Lazer. We were put in a newly constructed two-story building and this time the boys were separated from the girls. Four kids shared each room. On the second floor, I shared a room with Ezra and Kalman to start with. Later, an orphan from Egypt showed up, Mordechai. They assigned a mother from the kibbutz to care for us. If anyone needed something, they went to her.

Ours was the first group of orphans to arrive at Yagur. It was a good-sized kibbutz with a population of 1,200 Jews. They had a metal can factory for canning goods, orchards of apples and grapefruit. And a big grape orchard for consumption, not for wine. They grew tomatoes. Corn. A herd of sheep and cows for milk. Chicken coops for raising chickens.

We were kept busy, day and night. Our second day, we began schooling with two teachers, Shlomo and Shoshana. A man and a woman. Shlomo taught us Hebrew and math, and Shoshana taught us the *Tanakh*, the bible. There was another teacher, a musician, who gave music lessons once a week. We studied Hebrew close to four hours every morning.

Back then, I mostly spoke Russian because of the time I spent with the Russians. And I spoke Ukrainian because of my years spent in Richk. And, of course, I spoke Yiddish. For some reason, after all those years on my own, I never forgot Yiddish. But the adults at the kibbutz hammered away at Hebrew. Even the mother that cared for us insisted we speak Hebrew, though she spoke all our languages. Overall, it didn't take long for me to pick it up. I remembered the Hebrew alphabet from my early tutorials with the rabbi in Koretz. For some, it was tough to learn. My friend Aharon knew a little bit because he'd gone to Hebrew school before the war. Soon Hebrew became our common language, even though we came from all different places.

In the afternoons, we had military training by the Palmach. We were taught how to fight with sticks, how to assemble and disassemble weapons. How to clean rifles and guns. We were taken out on missions to get accustomed to different environments. In the evenings, we had lectures and classes. Occasionally, somebody would come and play the piano, get everybody singing.

They gave us something we hadn't had in years: regular meals and a solid routine each day. We got up in the morning and brushed our teeth. Then off to the dining room for breakfast. Though we were welcome to sit at tables with other members of the kibbutz, we kept more or less to ourselves. For breakfast, we had dark bread, jam made at the kibbutz, and tea or cocoa. Yagur had its own bakery and the bread was always fresh. Vegetables we didn't have at breakfast. For lunch, we had a hard-boiled egg and helped ourselves to salad. The salad was mostly dressed with white vinegar or wine vinegar. Very little olive oil. They were controlling the olive oil tightly.

For dinner, there was vegetable soup or noodle soup. Perhaps an egg, any style except omelets. Hard-boiled, sunny side up. They served a lot of those. Very few milk products. On Friday nights during grape season, we got a small portion of grapes. We were young and hungry. A lot of us were malnourished. Sometimes we helped ourselves to two servings. We were only allowed one egg but sometimes a kid would take two. Once a month, we had a small portion of chicken. Always hungry for meat. I noticed there was no blessing before the meals, no motzi. No religion at all. Only a couple of guys on the kibbutz stuck to their tradition by *davening* on their own.

Once we had stability at the kibbutz, kids started loosening up. Some were wild. A few instigators played pranks. My roommate Ezra was an instigator. These kids would put toilet paper between a sleeping kid's toes and set it on fire. Or they'd fill a metal bucket with water and put it on top of the toilet door so the bucket would land on someone's head. But that was just a few kids. The majority of us behaved well.

Of course, there were conflicts. We were each allotted one tube of toothpaste every two months, but a few kids used theirs up early and would take someone else's. Sometimes kids misplaced their small allowance and accused others of stealing it. Some kids tore their clothes and then that was an issue. I never had problems like that. I stayed away from the troublemakers. Always kept to myself and the few guys I was friends with. Over time, some of the troublesome kids were moved to another kibbutz and new kids were brought in. Mordechai, my Egyptian roommate, was eventually reunited with his brother. Another fellow had a brother who was also brought over. Certain girls were taken to other kibbutzim and new girls joined us. Our group expanded from thirty-two to forty.

In addition to school and military training, we were assigned jobs. My job was milking and shearing the sheep. I shared the work with a tough

Jewish guy from Germany. He was a *kibbutznik*, one of the pioneers. Very strict. He liked to have his independence, probably because of his upbringing, his exposure to a particular way of life. The German Jews were the elite, the most educated. They were looked up to. So even in the kibbutz, we had people who were looked up to and others looked down on. My roommate Mordechai was looked down on. Because of his curly hair and dark skin, he was called an Arab. He was the butt of many jokes. The irony was that he'd been orphaned by Arabs, when they kicked the Jews out of Egypt. I always got along with him. But a lot of kids didn't.

There was blatant disregard for kibbutz rules by some of the grown-ups. One guy tended a flock of pigeons. Outside of his little room where he lived with his wife and two kids, he had built a small cage. He fed the pigeons food from the kibbutz. Didn't buy the grain. Every once in a while, he'd take one out. Meat was at a premium. The kibbutz didn't slaughter cows or sheep that were producing milk. They saved these animals for production. And this one guy raised pigeons for his own need. He used to cook them to feed his family, which was against the policies.

When fall came, the German guy that was in charge of the sheep, he would take a shotgun and shoot quail for himself. Not just one, maybe a dozen of them. He'd come back with a bag of quails. I went with him a couple times, but he never shared with me. And every once in a while in the spring, when a lamb was born, this German guy decided not to report it. There was a book where the baby lamb was supposed to be written down and registered. Then get tagged. But this guy decided that lamb wasn't going to be written up or tagged. Because he wanted the meat. When the lamb got to be one or two months old, I watched him slaughter it. He had a deal with the guy in the bakery. After the bread came out of the oven, the lamb went into a pan. They cooked it and shared it. And the people that took care of chickens, every once in a while they brought a chicken home for themselves. Everyone else had chicken once a month. But the guy that was cutting and preparing the meat, he took care of himself. This was the type of thing that went on. We, as children, didn't care. But a lot of people frowned on these transgressions.

In the spring, my group was taken to the field to thin the corn crop. It was backbreaking work. The kibbutz didn't have the proper equipment for seeding and the stalks grew too close together. Our job was to kneel on the ground, pull up stalks, and shove them into a bag. Then we dumped the bags into a big pile. The extra corn was used to feed the cows back at the kibbutz. In the fall, we came back to the same cornfield to deal with the rats. The kibbutz made their own rat poison. It was corn dipped in a deadly red solution. Whenever we saw a rat hole in the field, we poured in a teaspoon of red corn. It was just us orphans that did this job. Not the kids with families. This was troublesome to us.

We were kept apart from the other children on the kibbutz, the ones that had fathers and mothers. They had separate schools for those children. After school, those kids had structured activities. Soccer, choir, social programs. In the evening, they would go home to their parents. Not only were we separated from these kids, we never intermingled with any families. Never invited to anyone's home. Never even saw what their homes looked like. So there was resentment. Not only on my part, but from all of the orphans. That was their mistake, the leaders on the kibbutz. They didn't integrate us. They didn't expose us to family life. And we missed that. Instead of family time, we talked among ourselves about the same old crap. Nobody talked about their past, what their families were like, how their lives were ripped away from them.

Pursuing education wasn't discussed for our group. We only learned the basics. Math, bible, Hebrew and music. Nobody talked about anything further than that. But these kids that belonged to families, they had additional education. They had coaches that came from Haifa and taught them athletics. Taught them how to run, how to play on a team. We had none of that. Occasionally we were thrown a bone, so to speak. If the kids didn't show up and the coach had free time, he'd be sent to us. After all, he was getting paid anyway. Some of us orphans were interested in athletics. Soccer was the game of choice. So once in a while, a coach came and talked to us. He never did much since he knew he wasn't going to be there the next week. When the boxing coach had free time, Ezra and I went. He coached the kids on the flat roof of the dining hall. The gloves were shared, since he had just one or two pairs. We spent more time watching than participating.

One day, the running coach had free time and came to our group. He told me one thing. "Eliezer, don't run with your feet spread out. Run with your feet straight. Because straight, you gain. When they're spread out, you're losing." Then he said, "There's got to be a system. You've got to warm up. You've got to stretch out. Otherwise you're not doing it properly." This was the type of advantage the kids with families in the kibbutz had and we didn't. If not for these coaches, we wouldn't have known about this stuff.

The Koretzor Society

One Saturday after I'd been at Yagur for three months, I was told I
had visitors. A man named Lamed had come from Haifa by bus with his
wife. Somebody grabbed me and brought me to the dining hall. Lamed
and his wife were sitting at a table. He looked about forty-five and she
was a stubby little lady. They stood up to greet me.

Lamed was a member of the Koretzor Society, a helping organization
made up of people from Koretz. He didn't know my first name but he
knew there was a boy at the kibbutz named Rubinstein. The society
had called him in Haifa and asked him to check on me. Somehow they
learned I survived the Holocaust and was at Yagur. We got talking. He
told me he was a good friend of my father's and had a gift for me. He
handed me a stainless steel watch. Then he showed me a photograph
of my father and I broke down in tears. I couldn't talk after that. Just
covered my face with my hands. He patted my shoulder and told me he'd
come back another day. He left the photograph and watch on the table.

In the weeks after that, Lamed came back. He told me he and his
wife left Koretz in early 1930 and settled in Haifa. I started to feel more
comfortable with him and over time we became friendly. Occasionally
I visited him. He had an iron shop in Haifa, under the stairs in an
apartment building. The stairs were the roof, the side was a fancy gate
that he made. He kept his tools there. His main work was making railings
for staircases out of iron, out of steel. It was the trade he brought with
him from Koretz. He worked by himself, the old fashioned way, and
supported his wife and a son. Upstairs he had an apartment, but he
never took me there. I'd only come and see him working in the shop.
His son was three or four years older than me. He had plans to become
a lawyer and a tennis player. Many times I saw him going to play tennis,
but he never invited me.

Through Lamed, I developed connections with people outside of
Yagur. He introduced me to a schoolteacher in Haifa I became close to.
Went to his house several times and had supper with him and his family.
He gave me cantaloupe for the first time. He had a lot of gadgets and
puzzles lying around. I didn't know such a thing as puzzles existed and I
was fascinated by them. I spent a lot of time putting them together and
taking them apart. This teacher was amazed that I figured out the puzzles
so quickly. He had a brother-in-law who worked for Solel Boneh, the
largest Jewish company in Haifa. A construction company. They built
homes and roads, constructed flour mills. I became friendly with this
brother-in-law as well. Who knew that later on, I'd come to him for help

with a job? The Koretzor Society introduced me to other landsmen in Tel Aviv. One of them was an attorney who had known my father. One had a wine shop. Another man owned a truck and towed cars for a living. His name was Yitzhak Katz. I spent an afternoon with him, just to see what he did.

While I was in contact with the Koretzor Society, I thought about ways to leave the kibbutz. I kept trying to connect with people, trying to network. Once in a while, I took a bus from Yagur. It was cheap. This was 1947. Ten or fifteen cents took me wherever I wanted to go in Haifa. Through my landsmen I met other people that also came from Koretz. I always asked if they knew anybody I knew. And one time I got lucky. Something clicked. Somebody knew somebody who knew somebody. One Saturday, I visited a family that had relatives in the Boston area. I knew that my father's mother was someplace in the United States, but I didn't know where. And I knew my mother had a brother Harry in the United States as well. My mother's family name was Weiner. Harry's Hebrew name was Arishver. Arishver Weiner. I remembered that.

I didn't realize how big the United States was. And I didn't know a city like Boston existed. But my landsmen put two and two together and decided to write their relatives in Boston and tell them they knew a boy from Koretz. That's how it came to my uncle, Harry Weiner, that he had a nephew who survived the war and was living in Palestine on a kibbutz. They gave Uncle Harry my name and address. We began corresponding. I wrote my uncle a letter in Yiddish and sent it to Winthrop, Massachusetts, America. I told him about the life I had. What I ate, where I lived. I figured he didn't know anything about the kibbutz. I described the situation, including the shortage of meat.

A few weeks later, a package was delivered to the kibbutz for Eliezer Rubinstein. It came from America, from Uncle Harry. An American Kosher box, measuring eight by eight by twelve inches. It was prepaid. A lot of stamps on it. And it felt heavy.

I was working in the field that day. My friend Aharon took the box because he worked in the office. "I'll give it to Eliezer," he said. Mind you, the box arrived out of the blue. We didn't have a post office at Yagur. Aharon brought the box to his place where he lived underneath the stairs. He had a little room by himself because of the injury to his foot during the war. He was like a bachelor there. Had the life of a king. He knew a lot more than we did because he was in the office all the time.

I came back from work that afternoon and he started teasing me. He wouldn't give me the package unless he was part of it. And what better place to store it, in case there's something valuable, than his room? Otherwise, I'd have to share it with three boys on the second floor where

I lived. They might get into it. He said, "You want it? This is the place to keep it. It stays with me." At that point, Aharon was no longer by himself. Ezra and Kalman had heard the news that Eliezer got a box. Keep in mind nobody ever got anything at Yagur. And here I was, with a watch that was given to me and a box from America.

I agreed to Aharon's conditions and he ripped the package apart. We saw amazing things. Midget salamis, six inches long and two inches in diameter. There were six of those and one big, round rolled beef. The package had been on the road for weeks and the salamis were green from mold. They had paper casings so the meat was protected a bit, but the outside was so moldy. And that rolled beef, with all that fat. The box smelled, mainly from the rolled beef. Even though it was cooked, it reeked. But we never threw things out. Salami we knew. We didn't know what that hunk of meat meant, though. We never saw anything like it. It was long and big, wrapped in paper soaked with fat. So slimy and moldy. But at that age, nobody was afraid of anything. We were closed up in Aharon's little room, no bigger than a hallway. The only place to sit was on his bed. Nobody had a knife. We weren't supposed to have them in our rooms. Ezra ran to the dining hall to get one.

I said, "Ezra, how are you going to take a knife?"

He said, "Don't worry about it."

Ezra came back with a knife so dull it wouldn't cut water. Never mind cutting a piece of meat. It was a regular kitchen knife. You could barely cut a hard-boiled egg with it. Well, we started peeling the greasy paper off with the knife and wiping the slime off the salami. We sliced it open and saw that it was green inside. But that didn't stop us. Aharon took a bite and said, "Not bad." The rest of us started eating it. We devoured four salamis. We could have eaten all of them but we saved the rest. And the rolled beef? We cleaned the outside of it and helped ourselves to the middle, which was the size of a salami. Most of it we didn't eat. Didn't want to get sick. Aharon became the judge and the jury of who got what. We said to him, "His slice is bigger than mine." The box was left in Aharon's room. Just like he insisted. He called me in every time he wanted a piece of salami. He said, "Eliezer, I haven't touched a thing. My hand is perfect." It took us two days to finish it.

There was no note in the box. Just the meat. Uncle Harry had told one of the workers in his factory to pack up a rolled beef and some salamis and send it out. That same night I mailed another letter to him. I made my friends contribute to the postage from their allowance. Each one paid a coin. The next letter that came from him asked me all sorts of questions. My mother's maiden name. Whether I remembered my grandfather. Of course, I remembered my grandfather, Harry's father.

I remembered my mother's maiden name. I remembered everything. I realized it was a test. Because Uncle Harry didn't know me. In my next letter, I answered his questions and explained everything in a clear way. I found out later that when he got that letter from me, with all those answers, he knew I really was his nephew. That unless I had lived in the house with his sister, I wouldn't know of those things. He revealed to me that his friends and family had told him before he did anything for me, this unknown nephew, he needed to make sure I wasn't an impostor.

A month later, I got a telegram notifying me that my cousin Ruth was in Tel Aviv. This was Uncle Harry's daughter. She had graduated from the Mary Brooks School and the trip to Palestine was a commencement gift. It was a group visit under the guidance of a rabbi from Winthrop, Massachusetts. Ruth had my address in Yagur and she made arrangements to see me. She came by taxi. Believe me, it wasn't a cheap thing to take a taxi from Tel Aviv to Yagur. And then go back the same day. It must have cost her a pretty pound. She spent the day with me, about four or six hours. I showed her around the area. Our conversations were broken. I didn't speak English and she didn't speak much Yiddish. But she realized there was a connection between us and we communicated in spite of the language barrier.

Ruth was in Tel Aviv for a week, maybe eight days. I visited her on a Friday afternoon. We went to the public swimming pool across from her hotel. I went to the bank with her, too because she'd run out of money. Couldn't believe all the cash the bank teller handed to her. It was overflowing in her hands. I had dinner that night in Tel Aviv and learned more about my American relatives. The rabbi that organized the trip spoke decent Hebrew. He translated and gave me a good picture of Uncle Harry's family. Told me about their meat factory called American Kosher. Told me about my cousins Sonny, Allen and Judy. And Aunt Shancy Levine, my grandmother's sister. That's when I started to dream about a trip to Boston. Finally, I'd found family. But traveling that far wasn't available to me. I didn't have the means.

Unrest in Palestine

When I first arrived at Yagur, there was a bus stop in front of the kibbutz where Jews and Arabs intermingled. They rode the bus together without any problem. The bus route went from Haifa to the Galilee or to Safad. Just around the Carmel. By 1947, relations began to get strained between the Jews and the Arabs, and there was a lot of aggression between the Jews and the British. Soon people were too afraid to take a bus. Certain sections of Haifa were all Arab, and Jews wouldn't wander there. Once again, I found myself in a place of conflict. I'd been in Palestine just over a year. Barely learned to speak the language. Before I knew it, there were skirmishes and fights and people were getting killed.

The real trouble began at the oil refinery in Haifa, where Jews as well as Arabs worked. The refinery had an iron gate with a chain link fence all the way around. One day in December 1947, the morning shift showed up for work. Some guys from the militant group Irgun drove by and tossed a bomb at a group of Arab workers, killing six of them and wounding forty-two. The Arabs began to riot. They surrounded the factory, closed the gate and attacked Jewish workers. Thirty-nine Jews were killed and forty-nine were wounded. The British were right outside but they didn't say a word. Didn't do anything.

That night, the Haganah got revenge. They came to Yagur and took a bulldozer. Three miles from Yagur was a small village, home to some of the Arab workers. They lived in little huts, for God's sake. Some of them straw, some just put together. The Haganah wiped the place out. They bulldozed everything. They killed men, women and children. It was a massacre.

The British came to Yagur the next day to look for the members of the Haganah that raided the village. But those Jews had left and even the tractor disappeared. They took off for the hills. The British didn't find them, but they found a cache of arms. The leaders of the kibbutz told us to fight the British with sticks. So we grabbed our wooden sticks and tried to harass them. The British could have killed us if they wanted to. They wore masks and started spraying mace. Tear gas. That stuff doesn't wash off. They hauled a group of Jews away from Yagur. Took them to the desert and held them there for a couple of weeks.

One of the guys from Yagur that was involved with that Arab village got killed. A young man, nineteen years old. He was part of the Palmach and used to train us. We all liked him. The group that fled to the hills brought his body and left it in the Carmel. There was a cemetery there, but the group didn't want to dig a fresh grave. The British would have dug him up. They kept his body in the mountain for almost a week and then buried him quietly.

By then, there was a lot of discussion going on at the kibbutz. The goal was to get rid of the British and establish a Jewish state. There was going to be a united Jewish army with tanks and an air force. Of course, for an air force, you had to have an airfield. None of us could imagine that such a small country could have this. There was a lot of political indoctrination. It was done discreetly at first, but then it was out in the open. Leaders came to the kibbutz and gave speeches about creating the Jewish state. Keep in mind that many different parties existed. We had the Haganah, the Jewish paramilitary, and the Palmach, the elite striking force of Haganah. And we had Irgun, the militant splinter group. Luckily, we didn't have too much contact with Irgun because they were based in cities. Most of us on the kibbutz belonged to the Palmach. Very few of us belonged to any radical organization.

Moshe Sharett was designated to be the foreign minister for the State of Israel. Sharett had an older brother that lived at Yagur. He was our music teacher and was raising two sons after his wife died. When his wife was alive, he'd worn the standard khaki clothes. But once she died, he wore only black. Gave us singing lessons dressed in black. We didn't understand he was in mourning.

Moshe Sharett came to the kibbutz one Friday night and made a speech. He told us, "We'll have a state. We'll have people helping us." That was the beginning of the independence movement. Once it began, all hell broke loose. The British sided with the Arabs. We were fearful of the Jordanian Army, only fifteen miles away. As part of our military training, we lay in ditches on either side of the road while trucks full of Jordanian soldiers drove past the kibbutz. We were scared to death. Didn't have any weapons. Just exposed. Those guys could have shot at us. But they never did. Some of us didn't want to wage war on the Arabs but it was a matter of survival. We were told if we didn't fight the Arabs, we'd be pushed into the sea.

When things turned sour, I was given a handgun. A 9 mm revolver. That was my protection when I went out with the sheep in the field. The German guy would hand the revolver to me and say, "Eliezer, take this." It only had three bullets, because bullets were scarce. I never knew if the gun worked. The German guy always took a shotgun. Believe me, he had more than a few shotgun shells. I used to watch him make his own shells. He had a machine that would pop the capsule, drop in fresh powder, put in the lead, put a piece of cardboard in front of it, and close it off again. Before I had the handgun, the German guy gave me a long barrel gun when I went out to the field. I'd stick it in front of my pants. It also had three bullets. Why three, for God's sake?

The attack on the refinery ignited the whole situation between the Arabs and the Jews. Soon the killings escalated on both sides. From a hilly neighborhood in Haifa, a group of Arabs began sniping at Jews. These Arabs had a good view. They picked their targets and gunned them down. People were afraid to go out the door. Anyone could be picked off. In fact, my friend the schoolteacher in Haifa, he was killed by a sniper. Left his house to teach one morning and was shot dead. Not more than forty years old. After the snipings came the revenge. A group of militant Jews gathered at Yagur and made their plans. Five from this kibbutz, four from that kibbutz. They had all the weapons they needed. The cycle of violence continued. Both Jews and Arabs feared for their lives.

Leon Rubinstein serving with the Israeli Defense Forces, age 19.
From left: Uri Lubrani, Leon Rubinstein, Moyshe Dayan, unidentified soldiers
Negev Desert, Israel, 1949.

War of Independence

When Israel declared independence on May 14, 1948, a meeting was called at a theater in Tel Aviv. Everyone gathered in the crowded space, talking and shouting, waiting for the news. Over the radio, we heard the announcement that Moshe Sharett went to New York and accepted the United Nations Partition Plan for Palestine. There was going to be a Jewish state. The United Nations divided Palestine into this section and that section. Israel was given 56 percent of Palestine, which contained 82 percent of the Jewish population. For such a small country, there was hardly any Israel. Still, everyone was cheering and whistling. Some were crying. Outside, they were singing and dancing in the street. Our excitement was tempered when we learned that the surrounding Arab states wouldn't accept the UN agreement. They vowed to wage war on Israel.

Israeli Prime Minister Ben-Gurion immediately created the IDF, the Israeli Defense Forces. He announced there would be no more splinter groups in Israel fighting one another or choosing their targets. The Palmach was dissolved right away. We didn't put up a fight, though some groups did. Irgun tried to bring in a ship with arms from France but the Israeli government wouldn't permit it. Arms were so precious, for God's sake. The IDF went out and blew up the ship.

The British began leaving when Israel was established. May 14th was the same day the British Mandate expired. They left everything for the Arabs. But the Israelis were organized. They grabbed the stranded equipment and tanks. Most of it the Arabs never got. Except for Egyptian officer Gamal Nasser. He came in with thousands of soldiers and took over a Royal Airforce Base near the town of Kiryat Gat. It was a powerful base and Nasser seized all the arms the British had left behind.

I volunteered at once for the Israeli Defense Forces. Signed up with a friend of mine from Yagur. He was a *sabra*, a native-born Israeli, the son of a member of the kibbutz. He was a year older than me. Told me he was volunteering for the IDF because he didn't want to stay in the kibbutz and be called. I decided to join him. We were the first ones from Yagur to volunteer. Me and my friend took a bus to Tel Aviv and registered with the IDF that day.

I never questioned why I joined the army. It was a risky thing. But I felt it was the right thing to do. I missed my family, I missed my home. Life was meaningless for me. So the atmosphere of patriotism, building a homeland, made sense. Also, I had talked to my friend Kalman about the military school for officers he attended outside of Peta Tikva. He told me how exciting it was to be at a secret location. The elite training he received. I wanted something to belong to like he had.

After I enlisted, I assumed I'd be placed with my friend from Yagur. But we were segregated because I came from Poland and he was born in Israel. I didn't see him again until I left the service. Didn't even know he was alive.

I was put in a special squad involved with explosive devices. We had only four days of training. Our instructor was a big, bulky soldier whose father was in the road-building business. So he had experience with explosives but he didn't have formal training. He didn't emphasize the seriousness of working with mines and explosives. The first day, he took us to an open field and gave a lesson on pipe explosives. We stood in a circle around the pipe. It was wired with a battery that was outside the circle. He moved back and forth while he taught us about the explosive. These explosives were set into three-foot long pipes. The pipes could be combined into six feet or nine feet, depending how much was needed. They were designed to be thrown across sharp, razor wire fences that protected enemy territory. The razor wire fence was like a spring, and it was stretched out. Once it was hit by a pipe explosive, the fence would collapse.

While the instructor was talking, someone in the circle went over to the battery and set off the explosive. And the pipe blew apart. Shrapnel came flying out. Mainly it was dust and sand, but rock and pebbles were also kicked up. A lot of us got hit by small stones, but nobody was killed. Fragments of that pipe were embedded in my chest. They kept coming out for a long time.

After that training, we were sent to an area near Kiryat Gat, to take over a hill and protect a nearby kibbutz. The Israeli government also wanted to control the airbase that Gamal Nasser's troops had taken over. Seventy-five of us were divided into three groups of twenty-five. The first night we marched toward our destination. It was pitch black outside. We carried our equipment quietly as we walked by Nasser's fortress. All of a sudden, the Egyptian soldiers realized someone was outside. They were edgy, those soldiers, and they had plenty of ammo. They started shooting in our direction. We could see the tracers flying. We dropped down, holding close to the ground. The tracers were all over the place. Some of the kids, it was the first time they'd been under fire and they started crying.

Then an alarm clock went off. We heard "Brrrring! Brrring! Brrring!" A kid from Tel Aviv, his mother packed his bag with an alarm clock. Fortunately, the noise of the alarm was covered by all the shooting. If the soldiers were smart, they would have lobbed a few mortars in our direction. They would have got us. We were in an open field, no place to hide. The shooting went on for an hour. They never came out to challenge us, but they knew something was going on. They were probably more scared than we were.

When the shooting stopped, we picked ourselves up and made our way to the hill. One soldier knew where to go and the rest of us followed. The next morning, the Egyptian army sent a plane to check us out. They knew we'd taken over the hill. Nobody had been guarding it. It was a strategic location, protruding a little bit above the flat desert. By the time the plane arrived, we had a flag there. We were digging trenches to protect ourselves so we could run from one place to the other. We set up a couple of machine gun nests. Put up barbed wire. Soon two more Egyptian planes appeared and they started lobbing shells at us from Gaza, which they controlled. They had heavy artillery. Most of the shells landed close to the hill. But we were dug in pretty well.

Our cook was setting up a kitchen at the bottom of the hill, away from the Gaza side. But that wasn't a smart thing to do. It brought too much attention. The pilots saw the cooking and lobbed a bomb into the kitchen. Two girls were killed. The cook that came with us, he was killed. Six people were killed that day. It was a mess. From seventy-five soldiers, six were gone. If we had had more training, that wouldn't have happened. Setting up and making a fire and calling attention. That was a no-no. The leader of the group asked for volunteers to bury the dead. A lot of the kids couldn't handle it. I went over with a blanket. I found a leg, a hand, a piece of a head. I put everything in the blanket. Dug a hole in the sand and dumped everybody together. We didn't know who was who.

Without the kitchen, we had little food. Believe me, nobody came to rescue us. We were there quite a few days. There was a fruit orchard about a mile away. We saw it with binoculars but were afraid to go there. It might have been mined. We kept looking through the binoculars and soon we saw Egyptian soldiers going to the orchard. Taking oranges off the trees and relieving themselves. We debated whether we wanted to go to the orchard and pick some fruit. A small scouting group was assembled and I volunteered. There were six of us. I carried a machine gun. We went there at night. Wasn't much fruit left on the trees and the area stunk of human waste. But it was a shady place. We sat on a hill with no shade at all. We decided we wouldn't let the Egyptians have this sanctuary. If we couldn't go there, why should they? We made a decision to mine the area.

Within a few days, supplies were delivered to us. Food and water, medical necessities. We had an ambulance and a couple of substantial,

American-made vehicles. Quite a bit of stuff. After a couple of weeks, we finally accumulated enough small mines. One night, we lay close to fifty mines in the orchard. Four of us went out there. Two of us were laying mines and two were watching. We came back to the hill. And sure enough, those mines worked. A couple of soldiers set them off. Once they were hit, the Egyptians never went back. The bodies lay stranded there. We could smell them.

Another day we were guarding the base at the top of the hill. An Egyptian vehicle drove past on the open road. We didn't have a heavy caliber machine gun that could reach that distance. Our machine guns were good for four hundred yards, six hundred yards. We decided to set up a trap on the road because vehicles were going back and forth. I went out there with two other soldiers and machine guns. When the vehicle came, we started shooting at the tires and right away, it stopped. There were six guys on top of the vehicle. They jumped down. Started running and shooting at us. Then we saw fire coming from our hill against these soldiers. The fire couldn't reach them and they got away. After that, we didn't see single vehicles on the road again. They always went in a convoy of two, three or four vehicles.

The Arabs never attacked the hill we were on. We were there for about a month. After that, we got reinforcements and spread out. I was assigned to a motor pool at a camp between Tel Aviv and Beersheba, mainly involved in transporting things. I was the only one in my group with a driver's license. I obtained it soon after joining the IDF. Nobody gave me a test. Just started driving and they issued me a license.

One night there was a fight in the area where the hill was. One soldier had to be evacuated and I was sent with an ambulance. I knew the back roads. But after twenty minutes, I hit a mine. The right side of the ambulance was ripped off. It was a British made vehicle, so the driver's side was on the right. I couldn't drive, I couldn't communicate. Just sat there in shock from the blow. The captain of my group knew there were mines in the area and he sent out a scouting group. The soldiers found me and carried me on the stretcher from the ambulance. I got some shrapnel in my chest, but they didn't attend to me too much. Most of the shrapnel was just underneath the skin. They put on some iodine and bandages. I recouped at the base for a few days.

Another night, my group took over a farmhouse in a small Arab village. I was sent with a truck to load up their sheep and transport them to a kibbutz. While I was driving, I hit another mine. Blew off the rear section of the truck. I was sitting in the front, not sure what to do. Soon an Israeli truck came from the direction of the village.

The Israeli soldier pulled his truck over and asked, "What happened?"
I said, "I hit a mine."
He said, "Come back with me."

He drove me back to the base. Somebody else was sent to pick up the sheep. Once again, I survived.

Yes, serving in the IDF was dangerous. No doubt about it. Periodically we had military training and sometimes incidents occurred there, as well. One time my group was on a bus, traveling from one base to another. In those days, the roads in Israel weren't wide enough, and this bus was driving on a narrow two-lane highway. Moving about thirty-five, forty miles an hour. The bus driver was on the left-hand side, even though we were still following the British system where we drove on the right side of the road. All of us soldiers were talking on the bus. Telling jokes, goofing around. The windows were open because it was hot.

A friend of mine, sitting two seats ahead of me, had his elbow out the window. After a while, a truck came from the opposite direction and kissed the bus. A scrape between the truck and the bus. And this guy's arm, it was chopped off just above the elbow. Fell through the window. It was his left arm and his watch was on it. The soldier stood up after he lost his arm and went to the front of the bus. Nobody knew what had happened. He said to the driver, "It doesn't feel good without an arm." He asked the driver to stop the bus because he had to find his arm with the watch. He walked off the bus and collapsed. Then we realized what had taken place. Somebody took a shirt and made a tourniquet. That stopped the bleeding. We all went outside looking for his arm. If it wasn't for that stainless steel watch, which was shining in the sun, we would never have found it.

I bumped into that soldier after the war and he was in good shape. He was functioning fine without an arm. He was a great guy. Good sense of humor. Came from a poor part of Tel Aviv. For me, it was traumatic to see him lose his arm. But the other soldiers handled it like it was no big deal.

Other things happened during training sessions. One time, we were practicing to cross the Jordan River using ropes. They stretched out a rope on the bottom, a rope on the top. This was high off the ground. One at a time we crossed because the ropes wouldn't support more than one person. After me came a soldier who started fooling around. Rocking back and forth on the ropes. And he fell off. He lay on the ground with a broken leg and was harshly reprimanded. And it struck me as funny. His leg needed attention but he was being yelled at.

One of the biggest missions for my group was Operation Uvda. It was March 1949. Well into the war. I was with the Negev Brigade, taking over the spot that today is Eilat. Nobody had ever explored that area and there were no roads to get there. We decided to make our way. We took four jeeps and two small trucks and an armored Israeli vehicle. There were seventy people in the Negev Brigade, well-armed. We first made it to Beersheba. Saw a lot of Bedouins living in tents. Some of the soldiers in my group knew how to speak Arabic. So we stopped and talked to them, maintained friendly relations. Resupplied ourselves and moved on.

From there we made it to the Dead Sea. Didn't encounter anybody. It took us a week and a half to make it to the copper mines. Constantly changing tires because of the rocky terrain. There was no resistance at all on the road to Eilat. We got bored after the fourth or fifth day, so we set up a place for target practice. We had a lot of ammo. Finally made it to Eilat. There was nothing there aside from a fishing shack. We set up base right away. It was dangerous because it was deserted. We could have been cut off at any time. Aqaba was across the other side, but the Jordanians didn't bother us. Nobody showed up. We knew it wouldn't take long before we established other bases in the area.

Most of my friends from Yagur finished their military service much sooner than I did. Since they were on a kibbutz, they were already serving the country. They didn't get drafted until the war was almost over. Served six or seven months at the most, after going through a group training. Never saw a battle. Once they finished their service, they established a kibbutz in the Negev called Mashabei Sadeh. Most everyone was there except for Aharon. He stayed in Yagur. In those days, the desert was a rough place for someone with a bad foot. When they first arrived, there was nothing. Completely desolate. They lived in tents. Then they put up a pre-fab building. They got a couple of cows. Pretty soon they had quite a kibbutz.

Prior to establishing Mashabei Sadeh, they stayed for a short while at a kibbutz in the Galilee. One of the guys, Shimshon Klakstein, took sick with malaria. The people that cared for Shimson didn't understand the disease and he passed away a young man. Twenty-one years old. My friends brought his body to Mashabei Sadeh and established a cemetery there. When they buried Shimshon they said, "We're going to have a kibbutz here in a month or two."

I visited Mashabei Sadeh when I was serving at a base outside Beersheba. The reason for my visit was that Aharon wanted to see Shimshon's grave. Aharon had been very close to him. He hitchhiked from Yagur to my camp in the Negev and stayed overnight. I slept in a tent. Gave him a cot. Our friends had been in the Negev only four weeks. I didn't know where the kibbutz was exactly. Knew it was someplace outside Beersheba. It was dangerous to drive. We could be ambushed. So

I brought weapons with us. I took a military jeep and a blanket because the jeep was wide open. I didn't have proper clothing for this type of trip. Aharon and I left that afternoon in the daylight.

When we got there, it was dark. First thing, we wanted to see Shimshon's grave. We took some flashlights and started walking away from the building where our buddies were staying. There were no more than twenty-five people there. Our friends heard us walking outside and called out, "Who's there?" We went into the building and they hugged us like brothers. Four or five of us went out and put a stone on the grave. For tradition. We didn't stay out long. It was bitter cold. In the desert it gets that way. During the day it's boiling hot and at night it's biting cold. The military provided the kibbutz with two tanks in the cemetery and a dozen soldiers guarding them. The soldiers sitting on the tanks were dressed warm. Spending the night on those hunks of steel. Young guys. I saw them shivering. The tanks were the most important things that kibbutz had. They were there a long time, until the kibbutz was well-established.

There was no room for us to sleep at the kibbutz. Not even on the floor. And nobody had any food. That meant no breakfast. I said to Aharon, "I'm not spending the night here. We're going back to the camp." Our friends advised against it. Too dangerous to travel at night in unfamiliar territory. But I said, "No, we're going back. I know the way." Now, this kibbutz was deep in the desert. It was no place. If somebody wanted to get rid of us, they could easily have done that. Aharon was scared but I insisted we leave. We drove all the way back to the camp without a problem. Entered the grounds and told the sentry who we were.

"Who is this guy?"

"He's a friend of mine."

They checked Aharon's documents. Finally, we went into the tent and we slept. Early in the morning, I arranged a trip back to Yagur for Aharon in a military vehicle. He was up before breakfast. The cooks in the kitchen, they knew me. I grabbed some food for Aharon. He was shivering cold. I had only one blanket. If I gave up the blanket, I would sleep without one. There was no such thing. But he was freezing and I felt sorry for him. He left to go back to Yagur and a few minutes later I grabbed my blanket and jumped in the jeep. I chased their vehicle. By then he was on the main highway, going 50 miles per hour. They didn't drive fast, those vehicles. I took a short cut. Raced through back fields and caught up with them. Stopped the vehicle. I knew the driver. And I gave Aharon that blanket.

Meanwhile, I had a military assignment back in camp. So I took another short cut. But I didn't make it. Got stuck in mud. I walked to the camp, missed my assignment. Was chewed out by my officers. They had to bring a heavy vehicle to pull my jeep out of the mud. They nearly court-martialed me for that. Finally, they hushed it up. I don't know what happened to the blanket. Never got it back.

In early 1950, I had another assignment near Mashabei Sadeh. I decided to take a side trip and see how much progress they'd made. Again, they received me warmly, like a brother. Gave me some food and showed me around the kibbutz. They had new chicken coops and more dairy cows, and they were making plans for a factory.

After the visit, I headed back to my base. Drove past a low spot in the desert, a mile-long stretch. When it rained, that spot filled up with water fast. Almost like a dry lakebed during a rainfall. Well, a wall of water came out of nowhere and began filling up the jeep. I tried to fight my way out but the water knocked me down. Water was everywhere. The engine was still running because it had a protective pan. I crawled and crawled through the water for half an hour. Then, as fast as that water came pouring in, that's how quickly it disappeared. One minute I was sitting in water and then the water was gone. I could see where I was going again. The jeep was still running and I made it back to the base.

By the summer of 1950, I completed my military service. After two years, I was out. The Israeli War of Independence was over. What marked the end of the war was a prolonged ceasefire. An extended period of quiet. But truly, until today, the hostilities have never ended. The war is still going on. I don't know how it will resolve.

Haifa

When my military service was over, I turned in my uniform, my shoes, everything. In those days, you left the army practically the way you came in. With your clothes on. My original clothes from Yagur were gone but somehow I got myself fresh clothes. I didn't have much money. The army gave a meager allowance. Mostly soldiers spent their money on cigarettes. Couldn't afford much else. These were tough times in Israel. There were hardly any single women to socialize with and jobs were scarce. The few guys that had work were making very little money. When people worked, they got an IOU slip. They didn't get paid right away. The contractor they worked for might collect some money in the future and pay them later. It was a struggling economy.

I didn't want to return to Yagur. My plan was to get to the United States, where my American relatives lived. But first, I needed a place to organize myself and make some money. I decided to stay in Haifa. My first few nights out of the army I spent with Ezra. He lived with his brother and sister-in-law in a house that belonged to an Arab family that fled the city. A one-story building made of Jerusalem stone. Three rooms, high ceilings. Ezra had one bedroom, and his brother and wife had the other bedroom. I slept on the floor, the coolest spot. It was summertime. Hot and muggy.

After a couple of days, I found another place to stay. I met a fellow from Koretz that lived on the roof of a five-story building. Another guy who lived inside the building had built a little shack up there. No more than six feet by six feet. Enough to hold one bed. He rented it out for nine pounds a month. My landsman who lived in the shack worked nights and I intended to work day shifts. We shared the bed. For the toilet, including the water, we went down to the guy's bathroom that rented out the place. It was an odd set-up.

At that time, Ezra and his brother worked together. His brother had a truck and they hauled bleach from a manufacturing facility outside of Haifa to Tel Aviv. After that, they transported vegetables, milk and yogurt from a main distribution center to local stores. Ezra liked to help himself to some of the goods. It was great for me, because I would show up and bring home a carton of yogurt. That was a nutritious part of my diet, with bread. Sometimes I'd get a carton of milk. Occasionally I'd help myself to some vegetables.

After I got the rental, I spent my days networking with my landsmen in the city, trying to get a job. I reconnected with the brother-in-law of my friend, the schoolteacher. This brother-in-law was a boss at Solel Boneh, the Israeli construction company. They were part of the government, involved in big-time contracts. Any kibbutz or city municipality that needed a building went to Solel Boneh. They subcontracted small projects, like porches and railings and sidewalks. There was an abundance of subcontractors who did those side jobs. Like everyone else, Solel Boneh gave IOUs instead of cash.

I stopped by the brother-in-law's apartment in Haifa and told him I needed a job. He said, "Show up tomorrow morning for work." There was no job interview. By 6:00 the next morning, I was on a truck going to a construction site. It wasn't even my landsman's site. He sent me to a project that he knew needed workers.

This particular job was on a kibbutz, building a three-story structure using primitive means. The little wood they had was strictly for forms. We hauled concrete on our backs in pails, up to the second and third floors. There was no other system. Luckily, I had a driver's license and was mechanically oriented, so my primary task was running a good-sized cement-mixer. I knew how to start the diesel engine and what to do if the engine wasn't functioning. When I wasn't pouring cement, I did the other work, like forming and hauling. Dragging up the boards or the studs. Tying things together with wire. The guys that managed the job yelled constantly if we didn't move fast enough. Or if we were grabbing a drink of water at the end of the day when we could barely walk. We drank the same water that was used to mix the cement.

My first day on the job, I wasn't prepared for heavy manual labor. Even though my landsman told me to show up for work, I didn't know whether I was going to get an assignment. I went there without any food. And I lasted the whole day without breakfast or lunch. When I came off the job, I didn't get paid. So I had to make things happen with the little money I had.

Most nights after work, I stopped by a store and bought half a loaf of bread and a few slices of stale cheese. That cheese looked like soap, for God's sake. This was my diet for breakfast, lunch and dinner. On a good night, I bought myself a cucumber, because they were cheap. Maybe even a tomato. On the weekends, the restaurants were running the same type of system the employers were. IOU slips. The restaurants wouldn't cater to you unless they knew you.

In Haifa, Ezra introduced me to a small, family-owned restaurant. A husband and wife did all the cooking. This particular restaurant also had a nice girl of Yemeni decent. I frequented this restaurant often. I'd go in and grab a table. No tablecloth, nothing. They wouldn't even bring a glass of water unless I begged for it. I'd order a cheap dish of potatoes covered with tomatoes. With the flavor of meat. Meat was expensive, so they used just a bit in the cooking to give a taste of fat and beef. And it came with some bread. If it was Friday or Saturday, I got challah. I cleaned that plate right out. Believe me, they didn't have to wash it. After I got through eating, I filled out an IOU slip.

Once a month, I got paid a few pounds. The first place I went was the restaurant and then the store that sold me cheese and bread. Paid them right away. I needed to make sure if I went there the next day, I'd get the same treatment. If I wasn't responsible, they wouldn't give me food.

One guy I knew in Haifa worked at a store that sold chickens. In those days, chickens came into the store alive. A shochet came to the store each day and slaughtered the chickens they planned to sell. Just two people worked there. The guy that owned the store and the guy I knew that helped him. My friend was married and lived in an apartment that was taken from an Arab family. Didn't have children. Everybody was holding off with children because they couldn't afford to feed them.

Occasionally on a Friday night, this friend brought home a chicken because it was left over. Nobody came to buy it. And I made it my business to bump into him on that particular day, because I'd be invited for dinner. He'd say, "Come on over. I have a chicken." Believe me, I wanted a free meal and some company at night. The place I lived, there was no company. No lights. I would climb to a dark little place and curl up to sleep. We never even changed the sheets because we couldn't afford to wash them. So when somebody invited me for a dinner of chicken on a Friday night, you bet I went. He'd tell me to bring a challah. Didn't cost much. He didn't want people to come empty-handed. Wasn't asking for a bottle of wine, because that would be luxury. Most of the time there wasn't enough chicken to go around, since this guy invited eight or ten people over. Too many people for one chicken. If I was lucky, I got a wing. His wife was a good cook. She did a lot with one chicken. Those Friday nights in his small room were packed. We laughed, we talked, we kibbitzed. Through this guy, I met quite a few people.

One guy I met drove a tractor for a living. When he finally got paid, he wound up with some decent money. He had a good-looking girl in the navy. A career officer. This guy was a heavy gambler and he associated with a whole group of gamblers. Card players. They started gambling on Friday night and all through the day Saturday they gambled, until late Saturday night. Most of these guys didn't have the money to gamble, but they did it anyway. I wasn't a gambler, but I would visit. It was a crummy place where they lived. Their house had belonged to some poor Arabs on Mount Carmel. The area where the Arab snipers used to live. One of the gamblers worked for the merchant marine. Most of the time he was at sea, but every time he was off the boat, he would come over. It was a social thing. Now and then, one of these guys would get a few bucks and they'd invite me to go with them to a sidewalk café in Haifa. We'd sit outside and they'd treat me to a soda. Nobody was drinking whiskey because they couldn't afford it. Didn't matter. We sat in the sun with our sodas. Watched the people walk by.

After a while, the gambling room came to an end. The fellow that drove the tractor committed suicide because he owed so much money to everybody. Shot himself in his apartment. His girlfriend found him there two or three weeks later, when she returned from a trip. That's when the group broke up. Occasionally I bumped into some of the guys on the street, but there wasn't any camaraderie. After all our time together, no friendship at all.

I worked construction for six months at Solel Boneh. Then I was called back to the reserves in an artillery platoon outside of Haifa. The military found me through my mailing address at Ezra's brother's house. I was in the reserves two months for peacetime duty toward the end of 1950. It wasn't a bad thing, because they gave three meals a day and had trainings. Even though I was stationed in the artillery unit, the only artillery we had were two pieces that were never used. The army was conservative as far as training with live ammo. I drove a truck with one of those two pieces at night, to get used to moving in the darkness without any lights.

One of my jobs with this unit was arresting people that didn't show up for military service. A lot of people didn't take it seriously. Or they were involved in jobs they didn't want to lose. We'd knock on doors and take these guys out in the middle of the night. Tie their hands behind their back with a piece of rope. Put them in the rear of the truck and bring them to the station. We were a back-up for the military police. Most of the time, these guys were just reprimanded. I don't think any of them served jail time. They might have stood in front of a military tribunal. I used to see the same guys we picked out at night in their sleep a few days later. That job lasted a week or two. Didn't like it at all.

In the reserves, I became friendly with a soldier named Aria Sobronsky. He was a handsome bear of a guy with a mustache. Looked like a movie star. He lived in a suburb of Haifa with his younger brother and parents. When he wasn't in the reserves, Aria had a small construction business. He handled the cement part of balconies. His brother drove a bus for Agat, the Israeli bus company. That was an achievement, because when you worked for Agat, you were set for life. His mother was a tough-looking woman. His father, he was blind and had been that way all his life. He had a little kiosk not too far from their house, and he attended to it as a blind person. He sold soda water, orange juice, candy, and cigarettes. All luxuries.

On weekends in the reserves, we could go home to be with family. The barracks emptied out on Friday nights. Even the cooks left. Aria felt bad for me because I didn't have any family. So he'd invite me to go home with him. First, we'd pick up his father at the kiosk if his mother or brother hadn't done that already. We'd bring him home and sit down to a meal of chicken and soup. From this little kiosk, the father hacked out a living for those dinners.

Where Aria lived, there wasn't space for him to keep his construction equipment. He had a small cement mixer and a few boards for framing things, and some staging for support. He stored this stuff at a rented lot outside the city. He didn't have a driver's license so he contracted out for somebody to move his equipment from one location to another.

Aria didn't have much work as an independent contractor, so he couldn't give me work, but he included me in his social life. And he had quite a social life because he had the looks. There were few women around but somehow he knew them all. They were young, nice, good-looking girls. Don't know where they came from.

We used to make arrangements for me to borrow a military vehicle for the weekend. I was restricted as far as the mileage. I couldn't drive too far, just in the city. Aria would arrange a date for himself on a Friday night after dinner. Just go for a walk with a girl. His best recreation time was taking a blanket and having me drive him and his girl to a spot on the Carmel. I'd let them off in a secluded place away from the housing area. There was open space there. I'd come back at three o'clock in the morning to get them. Most of the time, the girl came by bus and we picked her up in the city. Because I couldn't drive so far to pick her up at home. But I would always drive her back to her suburb outside the city. And that was taking a chance. I wasn't supposed to drive on Saturdays for personal business. If I was picked up by the police, driving a military vehicle without authorization, with a girl there especially, believe me, that was a no-no. But I took those chances while we were in the reserves.

Driving Aria on these dates was one of the things that came with the territory. But for me it was a treat. I'd go there Friday night, have dinner with the family and sleep over. Aria and his brother slept in beds and I slept on the floor. On Saturday morning, I'd take the vehicle and park it on the street near his house. Sometimes I snuck a trip here or there. Once I even drove to Yagur with Ezra to see Aharon, but that was gambling. Hoping not to be stopped at a police checkpoint. I was lucky. Never happened to me.

Another guy I became friendly with in the reserves was the cook. He prepared all the food in the army. We left the reserves at the same time. He was a chef at a hotel restaurant in a prosperous part of Haifa, on the Carmel. Occasionally I visited him, but I never benefited as far as food hand-outs. He was closely watched. All the food stayed in the hotel.

After I left the reserves, I felt pretty low. Without any capital. Always searching for my next meal. Occasionally I had enough change in my pocket for bus fare to visit Aharon at Yagur. I'd stop by there and get a free meal in the dining room. It was such a struggle for me just to get a meal in those days. Often I went hungry. I was envious of my landsmen who were more successful than me. Like Eli Gluzband. A handsome guy with a mustache and his girlfriend Eta on his arm. He wore a round hat and walked with a cigarette hanging from his mouth. Because that was fashionable. He'd take out a pack of brand-name cigarettes and show me they were made in England. Even though he probably only had one the whole day. But to him it was a sign that he made it.

On a Saturday, it was common for these prosperous guys, no matter where they lived, to come to the city. They'd take a walk and stop at a kiosk. Buy themselves a glass of fresh pressed orange juice, which was the ultimate luxury. Then take in a movie at the theater, another luxury. Unlike me, Eli had a brother and sister and his father with him to provide guidance. They took over a house that originally belonged to an Arab family. When I bumped into him, he'd talk to me for a few minutes and look me over. Touch my shirt to see if it was made of junk. Check if it was clean. Or if it was a shirt I wore for the last two or three months without being washed. Because who could afford that? I don't know how he did it, but he made it.

I wasn't the only one scraping by. A couple of times I bumped into a fellow I knew from working the black market in Koretz. He was shot in the back during the Holocaust and it was never attended to, so he was a hunchback. This young man really struggled. He lived with his uncle, another survivor. He passed away soon after the war ended in Israel.

As hard as it was, I tried to make the best of things. I was always interested in athletics, so I began training with a group that was part of the Maccabee, the Israeli athletic organization. They trained in a school gym with gymnastics bars and a weight bench. They gathered on Friday and Saturday nights. Never during the week because most of them were working. The first few times I showed up, I lifted some light weights and they didn't mind. I didn't have to be a member. Some of them were serious athletes but without supervision. When I was bored or lonely, I went there on a Friday or Saturday night. It was a thing to do.

After training, I'd walk over to see Ezra. By then, Ezra had left his brother's truck and had a new partnership with another guy. They had a cab and that cab was busy day and night. They had their own spot at the cab stand with a telephone outside and customers would call for a ride. Ezra worked a twelve hour shift at night and his partner worked a twelve hour shift during the day. Their cab was old and constantly needed work. But they had that great spot in the middle of the city. I'd go there after the gym and chat with Ezra until the telephone rang for a fare. Then I'd walk to my shack on top of the roof.

Next to my building was another building, five or six stories tall. There were no elevators in these buildings, by the way, just stairs. In the basement of the building next door was an orthodox shul. The members were extremely devout, almost like a cult. During the high holidays, they prayed and sang until the early hours of the morning. I would be in my room – more like a hole that I lived in, for God's sake – and it wasn't insulated. The walls were thin pine with corrugated metal on the outside. And I couldn't sleep because of the music. Most mornings I had to go to work early, usually four-thirty, five o'clock in the morning. I didn't want to miss the bus. At that time, I was taking any work I could get. Construction work, making steel railings for balconies, loading and unloading ships at the port of Haifa.

Since I couldn't sleep, I'd sit on the roof and listen to the songs from next door. They sounded so beautiful against the night sky. Sometimes on a Saturday night, they'd sing until two or three o'clock in the morning. Maybe they didn't have any place to go, who knows? At the holidays, not everybody fit in the basement and the service spread outside the door. A lot of people that had to work the next day lived nearby. But nobody said a word to them. It was just what they did.

Another way I killed time was to meet up with a few guys and run to the top of Mount Carmel on a Friday or Saturday night. There were close to 500 stairs. We'd make it to the top and look down at the city on a clear night. It was a gorgeous view. Above us, the sky was full of stars. Below, the suburbs of Haifa were brightly lit. We could see all the way to Akko, a city to the north. We checked out the ships at the port. Breathed in the sea air. On the way down, we'd run and jump four or five stairs and come to a landing. Then jump another five stairs. We never, ever walked. We were young, full of life.

One night, during the spring of 1951, I was training with the Maccabee. I was trying to make a maneuver on the parallel bar and I broke my right leg. It wasn't a clean break, but I didn't say anything to anybody. Just left the gym and limped to Ezra's cab stand. I told him what happened and he could tell I was in tough shape. He took me to a kiosk. I didn't have any money. He bought me a small glass of fresh-squeezed orange juice and told me there was no emergency room to go to. He said, "Everything's closed. But I'll help you to your room." It wasn't far. I sat in the cab and he drove to my building. Helped me all the way upstairs. He pushed me from behind, because he was small and couldn't carry me. When we made it to the roof, he said, "Tomorrow morning, I'll come back and bring the cab."

It was five in the morning when Ezra got off his shift and picked me up. We got to the hospital within the hour and the emergency room was packed. There were close to one hundred people there. It was the only emergency setting for all of Haifa. Ezra said, "Eliezer, I have to leave with the cab because my partner's waiting for it." Believe me, they hustled for every minute. They worked hard, these two guys. So he left me in the hospital.

The doctor didn't see me until three o'clock in the afternoon. Oh, it was terrible. My leg was all puffed up and I sat in a stupor the whole day, without food, without water. Compared to other people, though, I was really not an emergency. Other people there had bleeding problems, heart problems, you name it. When my turn came, they x-rayed my leg and showed me the crack. Then they put on a cast and I walked home wearing it. On the way, I stopped at a store, bought some bread and cheese, wrote out an IOU slip. It was late afternoon when I made it back to my place on the roof and I was supposed to be at work. My bed was not available because my roommate was using it. But he saw the position I was in and let me use the bed early that night.

The sharing of the room between me and my roommate came to an end after my accident. He got himself a job in the Negev. They were building a road to Eilat and paying the workers a bit more than the average wage in Haifa. He worked twelve and fourteen hour shifts and lived in a tent. If I hadn't broken my leg, I'd have taken a job there, too, to make more money. But it was dangerous, that type of job. People were in the desert without any protection, living and working in tough conditions. A month after he left, I found out that the tent he shared with some other guys caught fire. None of them made it out. Probably because these guys were so tired from their long shifts, they didn't know what was going on. Maybe somebody smoked a cigarette. Who knows? The tent caught fire and he was burned to death. I didn't even go to his funeral because I found out too late. It was a tragedy. Another one of my landsmen was gone.

I had the shack to myself but it was hard. I couldn't afford to pay the amount on my own, and there I was with my leg in a cast, unable to work. I looked for somebody to share but couldn't find anyone. After all, who would want to share that tiny room? I handled the place on my own for a month or so. My papers were slowly coming together to make the trip to America.

Bound for America

Throughout the time I was in Haifa, I corresponded with my relatives in Boston. I had it in my mind that I was going to unite with my family. I didn't have a visa but I had an invitation to visit. The big thing left was to establish the papers. But it wasn't easy. The United States government was working in cahoots with the Israeli government, and they weren't letting young people out of Israel, even for a short period.

At first I tried to get a visitor visa, which was nearly impossible to obtain. Then I changed the direction to a student visa. I said I'd go to the United States to study and then return. In order to do that, I had to be invited by a school. Uncle Harry was instrumental. He found a technical school in Boston that was willing to accept me. Eventually, a letter arrived from the school, stating I would get entrance once I came to the United States. I had no real intentions to study there, but that letter moved the process along. Uncle Harry co-signed that I would not be a burden to the State of Massachusetts.

Uncle Harry was a big help from America, but nobody helped me get papers on the Israeli side. I was on my own. One of the things I had to establish was a birth certificate and that wasn't an easy situation. Somebody came up with the idea that a letter signed by a person from Koretz would do the job. For this I utilized one of my landsmen, Lamed, the one who brought me the watch and the picture of my father at Yagur. His son had gone on to become a lawyer. I approached Lamed's son and told him my plans, that I wanted to go to the United States. At first, he wasn't receptive about me leaving Israel.

He said, "Israel needs people like you."

I said, "You know, this is an opportunity. I'm struggling here."

Eventually he agreed to help and drafted a letter in Hebrew, stating my birth place and birth date. My birth year I knew. 1930. But I never knew my birthday, so I chose a random date. February 12th. Turned out February 12th was the birthday of Abraham Lincoln, the American president. That seemed like a good sign. After writing the letter, Lamed's son went to a travel agency in Haifa that a friend of his ran. I went with him. Somebody there translated the draft into English and put it in the proper format. It was typed on very thin parchment paper.

Lamed was willing to sign the letter but he was living in Israel when I was born. I needed somebody that lived in Koretz before I was born, survived the Holocaust, and could sign that letter. Through the Koretzor Society, I found a woman in Haifa and she agreed to do it. She knew my family, she knew me. I found a notary public and got everybody together.

The letter was signed and it became my birth certificate. I presented it to the American consulate and they accepted it as an official document.

Obtaining the papers to leave Israel evolved very, very slowly. Took months and months and months. I started the process as soon as I got out of the army in the summer of 1950, and by May of 1951, the paperwork started to materialize. It began with a letter from the American consulate. Ezra was excited because the letter came to him, since I used his brother's address. I had no telephone so Ezra ran up through the city, from the bottom of Haifa, to notify me. He said, "Eliezer, the consul wants you to pass a physical exam with their doctor."

Now, my leg was still in a cast. It had been only two weeks since my accident. And the cast had to be on for six or eight weeks. The moment the cast went on, I worried the letter from the consulate would appear. I wouldn't dare go to the consulate in a cast. God forbid. I had to present myself in good health. One of the things I did early on was give them an x-ray showing my lungs were clear of TB. No way could I show up with a broken leg. Ezra said, "You need to be at the consulate next week. What are you going to do? You've got to pass the physical." We talked and talked. Finally we decided he'd drive me in his cab on the morning of my appointment. The consulate was in a nice part of Haifa. The plan was he'd bring scissors and cut off the cast in the cab. He'd massage my leg, because my leg would be pale. Then we'd see if I could stand on it. We borrowed the scissors from a connection I had. A fellow I knew in the army knew someone who worked for a guy selling sewing machines in Haifa. The guy asked, "What are you going to use the scissors for?" He gave us a pair of shears that would do the job.

There I was in the back seat of the cab on the morning of my appointment. Ezra cut open the cast. It was a pair of crummy scissors but he did his best. He said, "Get out of the cab." Told me to stand and see whether I could walk. I took a few steps but it was painful. "Don't limp," he said. "Walk with a straight chest and look healthy." He helped me take off the shorts I was wearing and put on a pair of long pants. Someplace we got a pair of sandals. I didn't have shoes because they wouldn't fit over my foot.

I walked into the consulate and had to wait a long time. I was sitting there and sitting there. A few times I went to the bathroom to massage my leg. To make sure it looked healthy and pink. Finally the doctor called me in. He said, "Take your shirt off." He looked at the x-ray, checked my chest. Told me to turn around. Listened to my lungs. Told me to drop my pants, checked to see whether I had a hernia. Then he looked at me and said, "You can get dressed." I got dressed and left. Didn't even know the results of the exam.

Ezra was waiting for me outside. First thing he did was drive away from the consulate so nobody could see us. We went to a quiet section and parked the cab. The cast was still in the back seat. He helped me take off the long pants and get into my shorts. Then he put the cast back on. Ezra had tape with him. It came from the guy that sold sewing machines. Ezra tried to tape the cast together tightly but it wasn't a firm wrap. It was enough, though. It did the job.

A week later, another letter came from the consulate. I was granted a student visa to go to the United States for three months. So I passed the physical. That was a major milestone. I kept the cast on until it was supposed to come off. That took another four or five weeks, and during that time, I didn't work at all. Didn't earn any money. I rationed myself a little bread and cheese each day. Most of the time I spent in bed since I had the room to myself. Ezra came over whenever he had a chance. And other people that I knew came to visit. They inquired, "What happened to Eliezer?" I wasn't a card player so we passed the time talking. By the end of my recovery, I'd take an occasional ride in Ezra's cab when he had a regular fare. Not a special fare. I'd sit in front and spend some time with him. It was boring but I wasn't alone.

Once I got permission for the student visa, the government couldn't deny me a passport. Uri Lubrani helped with that. He worked for Israeli Intelligence and when I was in the service, I was assigned to chauffeur him from Tel Aviv to Haifa. I drove him on the weekends to his father's house for Shabbat and we had a good rapport during those drives. When I needed guidance with the passport, I reconnected with Lubrani and he wrote a letter on my behalf.

While I was waiting on the passport, I stopped by a travel agency in Haifa. Told them I was in possession of a visa to the United States and was working on a passport. I asked them the cheapest way to travel to America. They looked up the schedules by boat and told me the cost. I wrote to Uncle Harry and he sent me the money for a ticket. Then my Israeli passport arrived. It was good for a year. Once I had the passport and visa, I went back to the travel agency. They checked the schedule and told me I could take a small ship from Haifa to Naples, Italy. I would spend two nights in Naples in a hotel. And then I'd pick up a big ship from Naples to New York. The boat leaving Naples was the S.S. LaGuardia, named after the mayor of New York.

One of the occasional jobs I had, before breaking my leg, was loading and unloading cargo at the port of Haifa. I got to be friendly with a clerk there. He was involved in scheduling shipments of citrus fruit overseas. The work wasn't steady but I didn't care. I was trying to get some money to buy clothes for the trip to America. When a ship came in, he'd give me a few hours work. Four hours of work one day, four hours of work another day.

When I finally had a bit of money, I went to the open market in Haifa. It was like a flea market, where people sold used clothes. I bought an old suitcase and a double-breasted blue suit there, but the suit wasn't my size. A landsman of mine was a tailor, and I took the suit to him where he lived in a suburb of Haifa. He fitted me with the suit in exchange for me securing medicine he needed when I got to the United States. He wrote out a list of medications that were hard to get in Israel. This tailor worked in Haifa for a small clothing factory. Their specialty was gabardine pants. Just the type of material for the Israeli climate. The tailor took me to the factory and I picked up a pair of gabardine pants for the trip. So I'd have a change of clothes. He got me a deal on those pants. And the guy in the port authority threw me a few hours of work so I could buy them.

I also bought an old, brown leather jacket at the open market. It fit me perfectly. My first leather jacket. I needed it in the port authority, because most of the work I got there was middle-of-the-night work. It was freezing cold. I had the jacket for only two weeks. The third time I brought it to work, it disappeared. Somebody took it. Couldn't afford to buy another one. This was during the time I hardly ate any food. So there I was at work, cold and hungry. The regular employees at the port authority, like my friend, they ate their meals at a dining hall. When my friend came back from the dining hall, he'd throw me a piece of bread and cheese. But I realized that food wasn't coming for free. He wanted something in return. He worked me for about a month like this. He'd throw me a sandwich and give me a few hours of work. After that, I broke my leg and didn't see him for a while.

When I recovered, I stopped by. By then it was almost time for me to leave on my trip. He said, "Eliezer, I'm going to do something for you. I'm going to buy you a pair of shoes." He knew I had a suit and pants. So he went with me and bought me shoes for nine pounds. And took me out for a cup of coffee with a roll. At the coffee shop, he gave me a list of things to do once I got to the United States. He had letters written to his cousins and addresses in the Boston area. He wanted me to check out the status of his relatives, find out if they were successful or not. He loaded me up with quite a bit of tasks.

When I was about to board the ship, this friend showed up to make sure things would flow smoothly for me. Ezra also came to see me off. He knew a bunch of people at port authority from his connections when he had a truck. It wasn't too crowded the day of my departure. A couple of girls were rushing by, calling out their goodbyes to sailors. I took one last look around, picked up my suitcase and waved to my friends. It was May 9, 1951. I was headed to Naples, then onto New York.

III. Young Man in America, 1951-1954

Map of the United States, 1938.
© Rand McNally, reproduced with permission R.L.08-S-63

Transatlantic Crossing

When we left Haifa, we had a real send-off. They gave us streamers to throw off the ship and everyone was waving and yelling. The ship was from Italy, so most passengers were calling out in Italian. Some spoke English. There were quite a few people on board. A psychiatrist with his wife and daughter were also traveling to the United States. The daughter was my age, a beautiful girl. They were heading to Bangor, Maine, where the father had taken a position in a psychiatric institution. He had a two-year contract, including living quarters on the hospital grounds. They had family in New York and planned to take the S.S. LaGuardia from Naples to New York. The same ship I'd be taking.

On board, they served three meals a day with plenty of dry wine, poured by the gallon from pitchers. I stocked up with some rolls and cheese to take with me for my stay over in Naples. With one other guy, I was assigned a tiny cabin below waterline, in the bottom of the vessel. It was a cheap ticket. No windows. The guy I shared the cabin with, we didn't click. He picked himself a lady when he boarded the ship, locked the cabin door and made out with her non-stop. The trip took three or four days to get to Naples and the whole time, this guy was holed up in our cabin with his lady friend. In the daytime, I couldn't even get in. A couple nights he wanted me out but I wouldn't leave. I complained to the steward about it.

We made it to Naples and I passed through customs without a problem. Near the port, I got my own room at the Hotel International, a dilapidated building in a low-class neighborhood. Half of the hotel was a whorehouse. A lot of sailors went there, people that worked on the merchant ships. For me, it

Leon Rubinstein arriving in America, age 21, New York, New York, 1951.

was convenient and cheap. I didn't have much money and it had to last the entire trip. When I left Haifa, I exchanged my Israeli pounds into American dollars. After the currency fee, I wound up with 40 bucks.

My second day in Naples, I noticed there was a barbershop in the basement of the hotel. And I needed a haircut. My hair was not well-cared for when I was in Israel. In those days, I had a big, full head of hair. I went to the barber and gestured that I wanted a stylish haircut but not too short. Had a hard time communicating because of the language barrier. So he showed me pictures of different haircuts. The American crew cut was popular because the United States had bases in Naples. I showed the barber the style I wanted. He put the bib on me and started cutting. The type of cut I wanted, some of my hair should have been on the floor. But it wasn't. For an hour he snipped my hair and still, I didn't see any of it on the floor. I paid the barber half a buck in American money. I didn't tip him because in Israel there were no tips. Even if I knew about tipping, I probably wouldn't have tipped anyway, because I was holding onto every buck I had. Every penny.

After the haircut, I went to my room to wash up. To take a bath. I started combing, and the hair began coming out. He left it on my head. Hair was all over my room. I didn't know what to do. Thought they might throw me out because there was such a mess on the floor. Like a barbershop in the room. After my hair fell out, I kept looking in the mirror and touching my head. It was the first time I had a professional haircut. In Haifa, I let anybody cut my hair. I'd sit in a chair and Ezra would do it, or if somebody had a razor, they'd shave my neck, and that was it. Now I had a real haircut and it looked sharp.

I went outside and smelled the sea air. I was a little afraid because I couldn't communicate, so I kept to myself. Didn't roam around the city. But I strolled along the street I was on, to check things out. There were outdoor food stands selling huge salamis and bolognas and big blocks of cheese. They also sold bottles of Italian wine covered with straw. I bought two of those bottles as a gift for Uncle Harry. I didn't know what they tasted like, but they had little straw handles and looked fancy. They cost 90 cents each. Other goods were available by the port, and I bought gifts for my relatives. Two sets of leather gloves for Ruth. I tried to remember the size of her hands. Cost less than a buck. For my Aunt Alice, I bought a cameo that came from Genoa, with little figurines in it. It was cheap, worth about three bucks. I didn't buy anything for my other cousins, Ruth's brothers and sister, because I didn't know their sizes. I didn't know anything about them. Just their names. Sonny, Allen and Judy.

I was in Naples for three days waiting for the S.S. LaGuardia. The first two days, I lived on the rolls and cheese I took from the ship. By the third day, I ran out of food. Noon was check-out time at the hotel and I was really hungry. The boat wasn't leaving until late afternoon. I walked around the area near the hotel with my suitcase. Dressed up like a businessman in my double-breasted blue suit. Some people were walking to a corner restaurant and I followed them. Looked through the windows and saw plain wooden tables. There was a menu posted outside but I didn't understand a word of it. I entered the restaurant and saw people with big mounds of spaghetti. I'd never seen spaghetti. Never knew a thing about it. Some had meatballs on it, some had sausage. I didn't know what those balls of meat were. The customers were twirling the spaghetti with their forks.

I left the restaurant and walked around looking for another type of lunch. A sandwich was all I wanted but I didn't see any. I walked past the outdoor vendors but they didn't slice what they sold. They gave out a hunk of meat and I didn't know what it was. It might have been pork, which I didn't eat. Finally, I got the nerve and went back to the restaurant. Took a table close to the window. The place was mobbed. The waitress came over and started talking to me.

"Do you know Italian?"

"No, I don't speak Italian."

She handed me the menu and I pointed at a dish of spaghetti. Just spaghetti with sauce, no meat in it. She motioned she'd get it for me, and she brought me one of those heaping plates.

I took a fork and a knife, and started cutting. But nothing stuck to the fork. I struggled with it. I wanted to eat it. I stuck the fork in my mouth and kept my mouth closed. Didn't work. I had a spoon but didn't try it because I thought the spoon was for soup. Well, there was a fat guy sitting nearby, watching me. After he put away his bowl of spaghetti, he moved his chair to my table. Brought his utensils and motioned he was going to show me how to eat the spaghetti. He pulled my plate over to him. Took his spoon and fork and demonstrated how to twirl the noodles. He ate it to show me the procedure. He showed me again, and ate it again. He ate and ate. Before I turned around, my plate was gone. I was left without a lunch. I paid for his meal and walked out of there as hungry as I went in.

That was that. I decided to stick it out and wait for the ship. Hopefully they'd serve dinner. Finally it came time. Took my suitcase and went down to the dock. The S.S. LaGuardia was a massive vessel. While I was waiting to board, I bumped into the psychiatrist's family on their way to Maine. We started talking and I knew I was in the right place. The psychiatrist spoke English, so that was a help. I stuck by them.

On board, I was assigned a cabin with four people. Again, it was way below deck, no windows. But I felt secure on that big ship. I put my suitcase in the cabin closet and started exploring the boat, a little worried that somebody might break in and steal the wine. The gloves and the cameo I kept with me. In the end, I worried for nothing. Nobody touched the suitcase.

The dining room on the deck wasn't far from my cabin. They served dinner that night and I loaded up with some plenty of food. I even took food with me from the table. At midnight, they served a buffet of sandwiches. Cheese sandwiches, salami sandwiches, ham sandwiches, you name it. Soda, coffee, tea. I could drink all the wine I wanted. Three meals a day. An ample amount of food. After eating, I visited the recreation decks. When the seas were calm, I'd pick up a game of ping-pong. I used to play in Israel, so I usually beat my opponent. It was a little tough because my leg wasn't that strong after the break. But I held my own. I didn't run around aboard ship. Mostly I stuck to where I was supposed to be.

It was eight days on the ocean until we made it to America. Coming into New York harbor, I saw tall buildings against the sky and the Statue of Liberty holding her torch. She was enormous, beckoning to us. On the boat, I had seen pictures of the Statue of Liberty at the information booth, but I wasn't prepared when we sailed into the harbor. The statue rose out of the water like she was waiting for us. We were greeted with tugboats to bring us close to the city. A fire boat was there, too, spraying water through the air. Maybe that was the custom then. I walked on the upper deck dressed in my suit. Kept looking at myself to make sure I was presentable, to see if my tie was straight. My heart was racing. Goose bumps all over my arms and legs. I was overwhelmed by the size of things. The statue and the buildings and even the size of bridges. Those bridges extended from the pier to the boat. We didn't have to climb ladders to disembark. We walked straight onto the pier.

We docked at nine o'clock on a Thursday morning. I said goodbye to my friends from the ship. Exchanged addresses with the psychiatrist and his family that went to Maine. My address in Winthrop I'd memorized. 93 Grover Street. I also exchanged addresses with other people I met who were going to different parts of the country. Nobody was going to Boston. Most people were staying in New York.

I cleared customs at New York Port Authority and saw Ruth with her hand in the air, grinning at me. A relief to see a familiar face among a crowd of waving arms. She brought me to Grand Central Station and we took a train to Boston that same day. Ruth spoke a broken Yiddish, but it was enough. I asked a lot of questions about the family, trying to get a feel for them. Where they lived, what they did, that sort of thing.

We arrived in Boston at South Station and the whole *mishpachah* was there. Uncle Harry, Aunt Alice, my cousins Sonny and Allen and Judy, the baby of the family. Sonny was four or five years younger than me and Allen was a young boy. They were all smiling and welcoming me. Such a fashionable family. Uncle Harry wore a top-of-the-line custom suit and beautiful shoes, and Aunt Alice wore an elegant dress and heels. The children were clean and their clothes were exactly the right size. Uncle Harry greeted me by shaking hands. No hugging, just a shake of the hand, and that was that. He had a good-sized Pontiac and we all fit in the car. We drove to Winthrop through the Sumner Tunnel underground. Never was in such a tunnel. After seeing New York, Boston wasn't as impressive.

Settling in Winthrop

The house in Winthrop took my breath away. It was a three-story building and a maid lived there, a kind, black woman. So many bathrooms and bedrooms! In the bottom of the house was a saltwater hot tub. Uncle Harry had water pumped in from the ocean for such a thing. I had the top floor all to myself. Four rooms. A gorgeous bedroom overlooking the ocean. My own bed. A dresser. Clean linens, pictures on the walls, rugs on the floor. Everything was immaculate.

Shortly after we arrived, we had a big, elaborate meal. I was stunned by the amount of food on the table. We started with tomato soup. Then a whole rib roast, corned beef, frankfurts. There were *knishes*, pickles, breads. Soda to drink. For dessert there was fresh fruit and cakes. After the meal, they threw out food like it didn't mean a thing. If it didn't get eaten, they dumped it. The discussion at the table was strictly about my trip and my life in Israel. They didn't want to get into heavy stuff. Just light conversation. Uncle Harry asked a lot of questions. "What is Haifa like?" "What is life like in the military?" Uncle Harry and Aunt Alice both spoke a good Yiddish, so it was easy to communicate. Ruth brought up the things we did when she visited me at Yagur. A lot of questions about the kibbutz. They were intrigued by that.

After the meal, I gave them the gifts I bought in Naples. The cameo for Aunt Alice, which everyone passed around. The bottles of wine they put in the basement because they weren't kosher. I don't think they were ever touched. And the gloves I gave Ruth, those didn't fit. But the talk was there and it was a long evening. Then the time came to sleep in this marvelous room looking out at the Atlantic ocean.

The next day was Friday. I slept late in the morning and woke up in my spacious, sunny American room. Too good to be true. I spent the day with Aunt Alice, watching her prepare for the Sabbath. Shabbat was a major event at the Weiner house. Uncle Harry came home early, and I watched him and Sonny daven together. The sun went down and Aunt Alice benshed candles. I remembered all of this from my childhood. Then there was another tremendous meal. Chicken soup, chicken with stuffing, rolled beef, salami, *blintzes*, *kreplach*, fresh vegetables, challah. Plenty of wine and soda. Cookies and cakes for dessert.

After dinner, I sat with Uncle Harry and Aunt Alice in the sun room, just the three of us. Uncle Harry wanted to know what happened to the family during the Holocaust. He asked questions about his siblings and mother. He knew his father had died before the war. I told him what I knew. That my grandmother was killed in the first slaughter. How my mother and father were hunted down and killed. How my sister Ana fled to Russia and the rest of my siblings were executed. I told him that Uncle Menashe was in the first group of Jews rounded up and killed. His youngest sister, my aunt who owned the ice cream shop, she was also killed. Uncle Moishe, the barber, he survived the war in Rokitna, Russia, with his two sons and wife. After the war, I found out he joined the Russian army to seek revenge in 1945. He took up arms against the Ukrainian underground and was killed during one of the missions. I told him that Uncle Yosef fled to Russia with his family. None of us knew at that time that Yosef survived. That information came in a few years later. There was another uncle who died as a young man from some kind of illness. I told him everything. There were big tears that night. Out of Harry's six siblings, five of them were dead. While they listened to the story, Uncle Harry and Aunt Alice sat together and held hands. They were silent. Completely shocked.

Saturday was my third day in America. I was invited to go to shul with the family and they introduced me to the rabbi. He didn't speak any Yiddish or Hebrew. Just English. I thought, "What kind of rabbi doesn't speak a word of Hebrew?" Then I was introduced to Masovetski, the *hazzan*. The cantor. He knew a bit of Hebrew. Uncle Harry introduced me to many, many people. Everybody asked how long I would stay. I told them, "I have a visa for three months."

Even though Uncle Harry was well-known, I felt strange at the temple. It had been a long time since I'd been to services. In Israel, I went only once, on Yom Kippur. A few of us left Yagur and walked ten miles to a *mushav*, a privately owned farm. They had a shul and it was packed. We couldn't get in, so we stood outside and listened to the service through an open window. It was the same as I remembered as a child in Koretz. Well, that was my only exposure to shul in Israel. And then all of a sudden, I found myself in this English-speaking. Conservative temple in Winthrop. I'd never heard of the Conservative or Reform movement.

The rabbi came over and invited me to read the *haftarah*. I felt uncomfortable and declined. Then I was called up for an *aliyah*. Because I came from Israel to America. And that was an honor. I was never given an aliyah in my life. Uncle Harry told me it was nothing to be nervous about. That there was a card with the *berachas*, the blessings, on the bimah. He told me I wouldn't have any trouble reading it. "Don't worry about it," he said. And I didn't. I was very good. Didn't sing the blessings, but I read them clearly because I knew Hebrew. After I got the aliyah, everybody came over and said "Yasher Koach!" "Yasher Koach!" Congratulations! Congratulations! They shook my hand. Like I was a famous person.

When temple was over, we walked home. The Weiner family didn't drive on the Sabbath, but it wasn't far on the boardwalk. Winthrop was a beautiful, seaswept town. The ocean was to our left when we were walking to the temple, and it was on our right as we were walking home. At the house, we sat down to another big meal and talked about me getting the aliyah. They wanted to know how I felt, and I told them I didn't understand most of the service because it was in English. We discussed it. The family wasn't quiet about these things. Uncle Harry tried to tell me it was not a simple thing to get an aliyah in this particular temple. They made a big deal about it. I joked with him, made light of it. I said, "After all, how often do you have a nephew visit from Israel?"

Once again, the meal being served was overwhelming. The main course was a whole brisket from American Kosher, Uncle Harry's factory. He brought it home unfinished, and the maid finished it off in the oven. Since they didn't light a fire on the Sabbath, the maid heated up the food and served it. Along with the brisket, there were other meats, side dishes and salads. After the Saturday meal, the activities were quiet. It was a Sabbath-observant family. A lot of books and magazines in the house. Uncle Harry took a nap, but most of the family sat and read. They subscribed to *Life Magazine* and I flipped through the pages. There were photographs of the Dalai Lama in the Himalayas and women in tight-fitting, red nylon bathing suits. Things I didn't know existed.

The next day was Sunday. In the morning, Uncle Harry put on *tefillin* and he and Sonny prayed together. Then he took his car and went into the factory. He came back by 11:30 with bags and bags of meat. Corned beef, rolled beef, pastrami slices, salami slices. Every kind of meat. They opened up a long table and set out piles of meat, platters of noodles, kugels and grains. Pickles and relishes. Vegetable salads. Stacks of china plates and silverware rolled in napkins. And all sorts of treats. Aunt Alice baked brownies, cakes, tarts, cookies. Pastries and rolls they sent in from the bakery. Freshly baked. And they put out soda bottles. The fanciest spread yet.

Then the cars showed up. Ruth's fiancée, Lenny Small, and his family arrived. Cousin Bob Levine and his family showed up from Dorchester, including his brother-in-law, Kenny the butcher. I met Aunt Alice's sister with her husband and daughter. Even the rabbi showed up with his wife, and the cantor with his wife. I'm telling you, there was a real crowd and a table piled high with food. When I first saw the food, I said, "What is this? A wedding? How many people are going to be here?" Uncle Harry said, "Oh, we invited a few people."

They had seventy-five or eighty people that first Sunday. All came to see me. Oh, the amount of people. The Kolka family from Koretz was there. They were distant cousins in the construction business. The father built most of the triple deckers in Dorchester. They're buried now at the Koretz cemetery. Aunt Shancy, my grandmother's sister, came with her husband Abraham, a tailor at Jordan Marsh. Uncle Harry sent somebody to pick them up, because Aunt Shancy always came by car. Never by train. Everyone else from the city took the train to East Boston, then a bus to Winthrop. But Aunt Shancy was a fairly old lady at that time. And I met the Penns that night, family friends. The father dressed like a movie star and the mother was heavyset. I met most of the Penn children. Hilda, Sadie and Arthur.

The old-timers spoke Yiddish. The Kolka family, Bob Levine's father and mother, Aunt Alice's sister and her husband, they all spoke it. So I had many people to talk to. A lot of questioning back and forth. Of course, when they spoke English I didn't understand what they were saying. But it didn't seem like they were talking about me. Some people chatted about Ruth's upcoming wedding. A few people asked Uncle Harry if he checked to make sure I was really his nephew, but most people were just happy to see me. Soon after, I learned that this type of party for extended family happened every weekend.

My first Monday, Uncle Harry brought me to American Kosher at 25 John Street in Boston. Showed me around the factory. It smelled appetizing, of cooked meats and spices. He owned numerous machines that manufactured every kind of kosher meat. Sausages, frankfurts, salamis, brisket, corned beef. The machines were loud and he had to shout over the noise so I could hear him. Told me he had four or five trucks on the road every day, making deliveries. At six in the morning, workers would start loading the trucks. Each salesman had a different route to delicatessens and small restaurants. He also showed me the books for his substantial wholesale business, where he shipped meat out of state.

Then he introduced me to the workers. They wiped their hands on their aprons and shook my hand. Or they smiled and nodded their heads if their hands were tied. His number one guy was Joe Ordman. Big guy, lived in Quincy. He was in charge of manufacturing salamis. Another guy was in charge of manufacturing hot dogs. Someone else was in charge of pickling briskets for corned beef. And then a large group of people were taking meat off the bones. His nephew Bob Levine and Sumner Kaplan both worked in the office. Sumner was the bookkeeper and Bob was in charge of shipping. Bob was also responsible for unlocking the doors in the morning and locking the place up at night. He put in close to fourteen, sixteen hours a day. He had just come back from serving in the army, and the job at American Kosher was available. So he took it. Aunt

Alice worked in the office, too. She double-checked the books and took care of the paperwork. Uncle Harry wasn't involved in manufacturing at all. He oversaw the facility and barked orders.

After the tour, Uncle Harry put me on a rolled beef rolling machine. Showed me how to use it. Took a slab of beef from the curing barrel and put a square shaped rod through it. Like a skewer. He attached the beef with a hook so it wouldn't turn on the rod. Then he started spinning the handle on the side of the machine until the beef was rolled into a log. Took the log off the rod and hung it in the smoker where it was cooked. This was done with one slab of beef at a time. Now, those slabs weighed close to ten or twelve pounds. Handling the meat was a lot of work. But it didn't take long to learn how to use the machine.

That first week, my production was so great I collapsed from exhaustion. I was a young man, twenty-one years old, but my muscles weren't adapted to that type of work. One fainting episode didn't stop me from working, though. Besides rolling the rolled beef, I packaged salami and hot dogs. There were two types of salami. One-pounders were called midget salamis and five-pounders were long salamis. There were different sizes of hot dogs, too, and they went into color-coded boxes. I moved salami and hot dogs off the rack into ten-pound boxes. Each box was tied with a string and then five boxes were packed into fifty-pound cartons. That's what went out to customers. The cartons were ready for the trucks every morning.

There were eight or ten refugees from Europe who worked at the factory and spoke only Yiddish. They stuck it out together because they couldn't communicate with anybody else. I used to speak Yiddish with them. And there was a group of immigrants from Poland that only spoke Polish. They stayed together and so did the guys from Italy. Uncle Harry somehow had a way to communicate with everyone. Of course, the work wasn't complicated. Uncle Harry was very precise the way he taught the workers. Even washing tables was an art with him. The workers had to do it his way. They couldn't just grab a rag and start cleaning. If somebody was cutting meat a certain way he learned from another factory, Uncle Harry wasn't happy about it. His way was the only way.

The first time I swept the floor, he came over to me and showed me the proper way to sweep. "Hold the broom this way." "Do the strokes in this direction and then that direction." The first time I rolled a barrel full of beef, he told me, "You've got to do it this way or you're going to hurt yourself." Just lifting a hunk of beef off the rack, well, there was a way to do that. And if you didn't listen, he'd yell, "You better listen, because that's the way it's done." He, himself, never learned from anybody else. Some of his workers came from larger factories and these guys actually had a better system. But he dismissed it. He even argued with people that had been working for him many, many years. He would argue about the taste of a meat on a particular day, even though the worker was following his recipe. Uncle Harry would pick a salami off the rack when it came out of the oven. He'd cut it in quarters and take a taste. He'd start yelling, "You have too much salt!" "You have too much pepper!" "You don't have enough of this." And the worker would say, "Look, I'm following your recipe." That's the way he was.

When I started working in the factory, I kept the same hours as Uncle Harry. Twelve, fourteen hour days. He went in early in the morning, around 6:00 or 6:30 and stayed until 8:00 at night. Sometimes longer. If a truck showed up with meat, he'd stay to oversee the unloading of it. Many mornings, he'd be tired and I'd drive the car, even though I didn't have an American driver's license. My first week, we commuted together because I didn't know how to take public transportation. My second week, I took public transportation back to Winthrop on my own. Uncle Harry was tied up with a meeting and he needed the car. It was kind of a thrill for me, stepping into the subway car, then getting off at the right stop and finding the bus to Winthrop.

Uncle Harry and I would come back from the factory and the whole family would be waiting for supper. We'd bring home the main part of the meal. Forty lamb chops. How many of those can a person eat? I'd eat four of them. Or Uncle Harry would bring a whole liver, which weighed close to fifteen pounds. He sliced it thick, so each piece weighed over a pound. Maybe a pound and a half. He also brought home one-inch thick rib steaks. We ate huge amounts of meat every night, which was unbelievable for me, since I had barely enough food in Israel. Fish we never ate. It was very cheap in those days. That was poor people's food.

The American Lifestyle

The Weiner house was full of activity at the time of my visit. Ruth was out of college, preparing for her wedding. Sonny was busy at high school, Allen was occupied with Hebrew school. Judy was a curious little girl, into everything. In the mornings there was a lot of bustling around, getting everyone breakfast and their bags packed for school.

Everyone was involved with planning Ruth's wedding. It was going to be an elaborate event. I was asked to be an usher, but I couldn't fathom what they were asking me to do. I never attended a wedding, never mind knowing what an usher did. They told me they'd take me to a place and rent a tuxedo for me. Whatever that

Leon Rubinstein, age 22, Bachrach photo studio, Watertown, Massachusetts, 1952.

was. They also went out and bought me comfortable shoes. Not shoes for the wedding. Those were rented. Just everyday shoes because the ones I had from Israel were crummy, those shoes the port authority guy bought for me in Haifa.

There was a shoe store not far from American Kosher where Sonny bought a special shoe for himself. He took me there and guided me toward his type of shoe. It was classy but didn't fit my foot. I picked out a less expensive shoe that was more comfortable. When we returned home, the family criticized the shoes. They said, "Instead of buying a first class shoe, you bought a cheap shoe."

After my third week in Winthrop, I asked Uncle Harry if I could go to school to study English. After all, I wanted to learn the language. We decided on the Berlitz School of Languages. Wasn't far from the factory. I could even walk there. Aunt Alice brought me to register and she paid for the program. The Berlitz School had private language tutors. Their system was for the tutor to guide the student in conversation and correct the pronunciations. For me, this method really worked. I had a month of lessons, three afternoons a week, for one hour at a time. After my first week of lessons, I began speaking English. My friend Jack Hershman always commented on how quickly I picked it up.

I met Jack the first month I was in America. He was friends with Arthur Penn and they came to Winthrop for a Sunday gathering. Evidently, Arthur wanted to fix me up with Jack's sister, Anita, who was going to Brandeis University. She spoke a bit of Hebrew. Jack's father was strict about her dating an Israeli fellow, so he sent Jack to check me out. Jack and I began talking and we hit it off. He immediately made up his mind I wasn't the type for his sister. He was a straightforward guy and disclosed this to me soon after we met. Jack and Arthur didn't speak Hebrew or Yiddish or any other language. Only English. And that was actually a help for me. I spoke so many languages. Hebrew, Yiddish, Russian and Polish. But English was the thing I had to learn if I wanted to communicate with these guys. It was English or forget it.

Jack was three years older than me and had just returned from military service in Japan. He knew everything about Hiroshima and Nagasaki and had visited all those places. An interesting background. Somebody good to talk to. He worked for his father in a small luncheonette, a cozy breakfast place. His father opened at four in the morning and they closed by 11:00 a.m. They had a regular clientele and made a nice living, Jack and his father. Their luncheonette was just a block away from American Kosher. Jack would stop by the factory and buy second-hand products for the luncheonette. He'd spend ten bucks and walk away with a carton of beef. They'd mix it with eggs and use it for sandwiches. Their luncheonette was open until 1956, when the Central Artery was built and the building came down.

Jack had an Oldsmobile, nearly new. After I was in Winthrop for two months, he encouraged me to get my driver's license through the Department of Motor Vehicles. One afternoon, he picked up an application for me and we practiced questions from the driving booklet. It was a verbal test I had to pass. The next day, I had an appointment at the DMV for the driving test. It cost between five and seven dollars and I asked Uncle Harry for the money. Told him I was going to get a license and showed him the application.

Uncle Harry asked me, "What makes you think you're going to pass the test? You've got to study for that. It's not a simple thing. If you don't pass, I lose the money."

So I said to him, "I've done that already. I studied for the test."

He asked, "Who are you going to go with?"

"Jack."

"Which car are you going to use?"

"Jack's."

"You've never driven that car. It's different than my car."

Actually, both of the cars were shift cars and I knew I could drive either one. In those days, the shift mechanism was attached to the steering wheel. Piece of cake. The conversation went back and forth until finally Uncle Harry took out seven dollars. The following day, I passed the test with flying colors. Afterwards, Jack dropped me off in Winthrop. I didn't mention anything to the family at supper that night. Even to Aunt Alice, I didn't mention that, by the way, I passed a driving test today. Instead, I sat at the table and the conversation went on about the kids and school and everything else.

Then Uncle Harry turned to me and asked, "How did you make out with your license test?"

I said, "I passed it."

Surprised, he asked, "Just like that?"

"Yes, just like that." I took out my wallet and showed him my temporary license. The DMV was going to send me the real license in the mail later on. He looked at it and shrugged. Nothing said like "Good job." Nothing said at all.

After I got the temporary license, Uncle Harry put me to work chauffeuring him around. Before I got the license, he was a bit hesitant for me to drive. But then it became a steady thing. In fact, I drove a factory truck for one of the salesmen who lost his license. I would load up the truck with him in the morning and go out on the route. He would do the sales, but I was the driver.

I also drove Uncle Harry to the kosher slaughterhouses he did business with. One was in Somerville and the other in Worcester. I didn't know how to get to these places and Uncle Harry wasn't so good with directions. But in the Israeli army, I learned how to read maps. The American map was different than an Israeli map, but I said to myself, "I can do this." I found Winthrop and Worcester and Somerville on the map, and I drove Uncle Harry without a problem. The slaughterhouses were cold, open warehouses with bloody hunks of beef hanging from hooks. I walked in and saw cows cut in half and massive slabs of meat. Blood was everywhere and the heat from the slaughtered cows gave a bad smell. They used barrels of salt to make the meat kosher. The supervisors wore white coats and the workers walked around with two-foot knives and plastic aprons.

During those first months at the factory, I became friendly with the workers, especially the Jewish crowd. Even some of the non-Jews invited me to their homes for social events. I went to Max the butcher's house, and Joe Ordman's house, the guy that made the salamis, and Mr. Kates' house. He was a religious man. Those days they all lived in Dorchester. When I went to visit Jack, I'd stop by and say hello. I knew exactly where they lived.

It was around that time I changed my name from Eliezer to Leon. It was discussed over a Friday night dinner. The Weiners felt uncomfortable with my name and it was hard for the younger children, Allen and Judy, to pronounce. So I changed it to Leon. It wasn't a big deal. After all, I'd had so many names already. Lazer, Vasili, Eliezer. What difference was another name? Sonny's given name was Leon as well, but that worked out because everyone called him by his nickname.

Soon after I changed my name, Ruth got married. Six hundred guests at the John Hancock building in Boston. I was an usher, I wore a tuxedo. And I was given a gift. A pair of gold cufflinks. Even though I'd never been to a wedding, I was a hit. I danced more than anybody else and I had more fun than anybody else. Maybe because I was missing out for all those years.

My social life back then revolved around Jack's social life. He was dating a lot and he'd bring me to dances to meet girls. Dances were popular on a Saturday night. Just a Jewish crowd. No way could you bring a gentile. There were people keeping an eye on that. Some dances were at hotels, like the Bradford Hotel on Tremont Street in Boston. They had a live orchestra. There was another hotel in Newton, where the Marriott is now, right on the Charles River. Other dances were held in Jewish Community Centers and there'd be a disc jockey playing records.

After the dances, we'd take the girls to a deli, which were social gathering places. The fashionable one in Dorchester was called G&G Deli. On any given night you'd go there and see a young crowd drinking coffee or tea. And there was a popular place called Jack and Marion in Brookline on Harvard Street. Another way we'd socialize was by getting together over somebody's house. One girl would be in charge of bringing other girls over. And maybe I'd be in charge of bringing some fellows over. We'd gather six or eight couples in a house. Play some music, dance. Have soft drinks.

A typical weekend I'd spend over Jack's house would start with Friday night dinner. Everybody would be there. Jack, his father, mother, brother who was going to medical school, his brother's wife, his sister Anita, and maybe a friend she brought from Brandeis. It was a traditional Shabbat meal. Jack's mother served chicken soup and a dish called *patchier*, which was made from bone marrow and garlic. It had the consistency of jello, but was loaded with garlic. We ate it with challah. Couldn't eat it straight, there was so much garlic in it. Jack loved it, because this was something his mother specialized in. And I knew about that dish because my mother used to make it. So we'd help ourselves to patchier and stink from garlic.

After dinner, Anita didn't go out because she kept the Sabbath. She had friends she spent the time with. Maybe they took a walk, read a few books. But Jack and I used to go to the movie theater on Blue Hill Avenue. It was called the Oriental. The ceiling had little lights that flashed on and off. Almost like a star ceiling. With the lights down, it was a magnificent place. It was a standard thing on a Friday night to have a Shabbat meal and rush off to the movies. And very cheap those movies were. Once in a while, I'd ask Uncle Harry for a few dollars so I could afford the ticket. It was a young crowd, a family crowd, at the theater. Jack and I would get there early and jump in our favorite spots in the back. We'd relax in these cushy, soft seats. Like sitting in a reclining chair. We could sit straight and look at the movie screen or lean back and look at the ceiling lights. People would start coming in. At first, they would sit next to us or behind us or in front of us. But we stunk of garlic. So the people started moving away. Jack and I knew exactly what was going on but we didn't give a damn.

Another social thing Jack and I did was go to shul. His father was a religious man and almost every Saturday morning he'd leave early for shul. About 10:00 we'd get dressed and show up. Many times there was a bar mitzvah going on. If a family had a lot of money, they'd go to a private social hall to celebrate the occasion. But a lot of times the celebration was at the social hall in the temple. After the bar mitzvah, we'd head over to the party and nobody knew whose side we were on. They'd have a kiddish and then hors d'oeuvres. And there'd be drinks at an open bar. So we'd stay there and mingle and talk to the young people. Try to pick up a few phone numbers so we could get ourselves a date. We did that quite often. Sometimes on a Sunday there'd be a wedding and we'd go and do the same thing. Dress up, have some hors d'oeuvres, mingle with the girls. Of course, we didn't sit down to a meal. After all, those seats were assigned.

While I mostly associated with Jack, I also associated with Jack's friend, Arthur. Arthur was a photographer and had ideas about going into the food business. He was always busy, always talking big. I used to double-date with him and his girlfriend Gloria. He worked for a well-known photography studio in Watertown called Bachrach. Jack and I used to go there at night because Arthur would work late. He took stunning portraits of us. One of them was of me bare-chested. God knows I had the looks in those days. We'd stop by and say, "Oh, I didn't like those pictures. Let's do some more."

Leon Rubinstein, age 22, Bachrach photo studio,
Watertown, Massachusetts, 1952.

Overstaying My Welcome

All the while I was enjoying myself with my new friends and working at American Kosher, the clock was ticking on my visa. Through Uncle Harry, I met his cousin Morris Anapolsky, a part-time attorney. Morris was one of the relatives that showed up for Sunday brunch in Winthrop with his wife. He did small things for Uncle Harry, like his will. With Morris, I began exploring the possibility of extending my three-month stay. But nothing came of it. The ties between the Israeli government and the United States government were close. They didn't want a young man to leave Israel and not come back. Well, I never wanted to return to Israel. My life in Haifa was no picnic. Pursuing an Israeli education was not an option for me because there was no such thing as night school in those days. And to go to school without any income wasn't possible. Manual labor was the main type of work that was available to me, because I didn't have tools to work in an industry. The only thing I was trained to be was a soldier.

Once I developed friendships in America, I was determined to stay. Even though I had friends in Israel, it wasn't the same. My friends in Israel – Ezra and Kalman and Aharon – were orphans. But my buddies in America had families. Jack, Arthur, Sumner and Bob Levine, they all had roots. And that appealed to me. My mind was in America and my desire to stay became very powerful. I kept pestering Morris about extending my visa until one day he introduced me to a blind attorney who specialized in immigration law. Through the new attorney, I went to United States immigration and got an extension for six months. And then I felt a bit more relaxed.

My first summer in America, Jack and I vacationed at Old Orchard Beach in Maine. There was a big crowd that came down from Canada to vacation there as well. We met some girls, went swimming, walked along the beach. Jack became friendly with a fellow who was going to McGill Medical School to become a surgeon. They took a stroll on the beach and talked. Jack himself wanted to be a pharmacist and actually attended New England School of Pharmacy in Boston. But his father needed him at the luncheonette, so he gave that up. Anyway, when the vacation was over, we exchanged phone numbers with the girls and this fellow from McGill. Then we drove back to Boston.

Right before Labor Day weekend, Jack came to me and said, "I want to go to Montreal. I want to see that fellow in medical school and I want to see those girls again." So he called them on the phone. Said he wanted to visit and he had the driving route. They said, "Sure. Come for a visit." Would I go with him? Right away I talked to Uncle Harry. I said, "This is an opportunity for me to go to Montreal with Jack over the long weekend." Uncle Harry said, "Fine. Go." I packed the few clothes I had and my Israeli passport. I had about twenty-five bucks on me that I'd saved from here and there. Jack didn't have much money, either. He got a hotel room for us to share and we drove to Canada through Maine. We got to Montreal on Friday night. Checked into the hotel. It had a small, clean lobby, a staircase and three flights of rooms. We were invited to one of the girl's houses for dinner that night. The other girls and the student from McGill showed up, too. On Saturday morning, the fellow brought us to the medical school. He gave us a tour of the classrooms and where they learned to operate. Of course, there were no classes that day. But he had access to all those places and we were impressed. Saturday night, we went out dancing with the girls.

On Sunday, I went to see Aharon's uncle in Canada. Uncle Usher was the one that Aharon stayed with in Rovno after he lost his parents in the war. Aharon and I were corresponding at that time. He had asked me to visit his Uncle Usher in Canada if I could. So this was my opportunity on Sunday morning. For some reason, when Usher came to Canada, he became an Orthodox rabbi. I don't know how or where he got his studies. I went to his apartment and it was closed.

His neighbors said, "Oh, he's in shul. He's the rabbi."

I said, "On Sunday?"

"Oh, he's in shul every day."

I went to find the shul and sure enough, there was Usher. I was surprised to see him, because he was no rabbi. He was just an ordinary Jew. Well, I waited until Usher finished praying and then he headed home. I walked alongside him and talked about Aharon but he wasn't too interested. He asked when I was going back to Israel. I said, "Not for a while." He asked when I'd see Aharon. Again, I said, "Not for a while, but I correspond with him." And that was that. The conversation ended and he went home. I conveyed that information to Aharon in a letter. That Usher was a busy rabbi and didn't talk much. Aharon was really disappointed. Here was his uncle. Like a father to him. And he didn't want to spend time with me. "Did he invite you over to the house? Did he give you a glass of something to drink?" I said no, we talked on the street.

The rest of Sunday, Jack and I spent with the girls. We socialized and had a meal. That evening, we headed back to Boston. Our plan was to rest up on Monday since it was Labor Day and we didn't have to work. At the border, an officer checked my passport.

He shook his head and said, "Your passport's expired. You're not going back to the United States until you get a new one."

Jack and I looked at each other. I was speechless.

Jack asked the border patrol, "How could my friend get an extension on his visa but his passport expired?"

The officer said, "It happens. He needs a new passport."

He told Jack he could go home on his driver's license, but I couldn't. My driver's license wasn't good enough because I wasn't a citizen.

I told Jack, "Look, I'll manage. You go home."

Meanwhile, we had only enough money for gas. That night we slept in the car on the border. Jack took the back seat, I was in the front. It was cold and we didn't have any blankets. Slept in our clothes. Next morning, we made it back to Montreal. It was a holiday in Canada, too. Got in touch with this medical student friend and the girls for some guidance. Of course, none of them were familiar with anything like this, so they couldn't help. Then one of the girls told us that the fellow wasn't a medical student after all. He cared for the rats in the lab and that's how he had access to the building.

Jack called his father collect. Told him the story. And his father told him not to leave me. To stay with me until things were straightened out. And don't worry about money. There was a means to wire currency through Western Union. His father wired him fifty dollars and we checked into a row house. Those rooms were rented by the hour. You know, it was a whorehouse. I didn't want to call Uncle Harry to tell him about the passport problem. So while we had Jack's father on the line, we asked him to call my uncle and tell him. Well, Uncle Harry didn't give a damn. He was no help. Matter of fact, when I was in Winthrop trying to prolong my visa, he was hinting that I should go back to Israel. That I shouldn't try to extend my stay. I have a feeling he spoke with Morris the attorney about me. Discussions like, "Don't be so kind in helping Leon because he's better off in Israel."

First thing on Tuesday morning, we went into a place that specialized in passport photos. Cost a couple of bucks for them to take my picture. The guy there was familiar with getting a passport. We told him we had to expedite it and he guided us to the right people at the Israeli consulate. There, we explained my predicament to the authorities. They told me I should return directly to Israel from Canada. They'd give me a ticket. Which I'd have to pay back with interest. I told them, "No, thanks." Very slowly, for three days, they worked on my new passport.

While we were waiting, I went back to see Aharon's Uncle Usher. And the reception was just as cold. I told him about my situation. Why I was still in Canada. I asked him whether he had any connection that could help me. He said, "I couldn't help you, no."

It was late on Thursday afternoon when I finally got the passport. The Israeli consulate gave me a hard time. It shouldn't have taken three days to get a passport. They were milking it. I told them we had no place to stay, no money and all that. They didn't care. Sleep in the street as far as they were concerned.

By the end, we were running low on money. We had to pay for the passport and we were running back and forth. Driving a lot. But gas wasn't too expensive those days. It was maybe 25 cents a gallon. After I received the passport, we drove all night to Boston. We got in early in the morning and stopped at Jack's luncheonette. His father made us a big breakfast. Jack put an apron over his clothes and went straight to work. He was so thankful to be back. I walked to the factory and began working, too. I told Uncle Harry what happened. He was upset with me. "That's what happens when you run around."

After that trip to Montreal, there were serious discussions between Uncle Harry and me. He wanted me to go back to Israel but I wouldn't listen. I said, "Look, if you don't want me in the house, I'll find myself a place to stay and I'll go to work to make a living." He used to tell me I'd be just like the rest of the family. He'd point out his nephew, Bob Levine. "See what he's amounting to? Driving a truck and packing boxes for me. He'll be this way for the rest of his life. Depending on me. If the factory closes, what's he going to do?" He said Bob wouldn't have a job. I said, "You worry too much about other people." That was my standard answer to him. Uncle Harry wasn't too kind to me after that.

I tried to figure out why Uncle Harry was so set on me returning to Israel. For one thing, he was highly influenced by Ruth's father-in-law, who was a big contributor toward Israel. He went to meetings and heard about the importance of building up the Jewish state. According to him, a young person like me, who was not familiar with the United States, belonged in Israel. The other person that influenced him was Bob Levine's father, Hymie. He also thought my place was in Israel.

Aunt Shancy told me these things when I visited her and Abraham in Dorchester. She thought she had some influence on Uncle Harry, but she didn't have much. Her children definitely did not have an influence on him. Even though they were all educated. Her son Abe was an engineer. Worked for General Electric and taught engineering at Northeastern. Julius was a psychiatrist and lectured at one of the universities as well. And the third one was a pharmacist. They had excellent relations with Uncle Harry. But no influence on him. I used to ask them to talk to him so he wouldn't be so harsh on me. But they had no say in the matter. Abe guided me toward engineering. He thought I shouldn't spend so much time in the factory. He brought me literature on different programs.

Aunt Shancy and Abraham lived on the first floor of a three decker, just a few blocks from Jack. Their apartment was modestly decorated but extremely clean. She was fastidious. I wasn't too surprised when Uncle Harry bought the building for them. He may have been hard on me, but underneath it all, he was a giving person. Aunt Shancy and Abraham had lived there a long time before the house went on the market. Uncle Harry inquired about it at a real estate office. Learned that Aunt Shancy was going to be evicted, so he purchased the house. Aunt Shancy didn't pay him rent, but the other two tenants did.

After he bought the house, he shopped around for somebody to replace the roof. Lenny Small's father took the job. Uncle Harry thought, "Look, the guy's in the real-estate business. He'll send a crew over to do the roof." As it turned out, the crew he sent was Lenny and Lenny's brother and two helpers. When Uncle Harry found out that Lenny and his brother were hauling shingles up three flights, he got angry. This was his son-in-law. Lenny already graduated from rabbinical school, and the other one was at Yeshiva University, preparing to be a rabbi as well.

Uncle Harry learned about the crew through Aunt Shancy. She called him up and said, "What are you trying to do? Jewish people don't do this type of work." She started yelling at him and that was all he needed. He got off the phone and called Lenny's father. I was there in the office at American Kosher when he made the call. He really let him have it.

"What are you trying to prove to me? If I had known this, you would never have got the job."

Lenny's father said, "Sometimes you have to work these types of jobs. They'll learn something."

Uncle Harry shouted, "No! It's too dangerous!"

He took Lenny and his brother off the job after one day. Put an end to that.

One Sunday during the month of November in '51, I stopped by Aunt Shancy's for a visit. She put some food on the table and we sat and talked about what's going on. She was inquisitive. Soon it came out that she and Abraham were concerned that I dressed so lightly when the weather was on the chilly side. Abraham insisted I shop the next day at Jordan Marsh, where he worked. I should see him on the second floor. He would pick up a coat for me and pay for it. I showed up the next day and started looking for a three-quarter size coat. I felt that would be sufficient. "No," he said, "you've got to wear a long coat because your toes get cold, too." There were hundreds of coats there and I picked out a long camel-colored one. Abraham didn't have to pay for it up front. The store took it off his pay.

Apparently, they weren't the only ones who noticed I didn't have many clothes. I was still wearing the same blue suit I came with from Israel. I wore it to temple and when I went out on social evenings. Jack and a friend of his, a cutter in a clothing factory, used to talk about how I always wore the same thing. This friend of Jack's was always changing clothes. And Jack had a different outfit almost every other day. Well, I had nothing to change.

One time, this friend of Jack's asked me to come to his factory. Just to see what he did. They were on Kneeland Street in Boston, on the fourth floor. The factory manufactured suits and sport coats. I showed up there on a Monday. And it was really something. There were long tables piled with layers and layers of different materials. Stacked up a foot high. This fellow showed me a pattern and traced it on material with white chalk. He used vertical knife cutters. Almost like a saw. He cut out sleeves. Cut out backs and fronts of jackets. Cut out pants. He was my age. And this was what he did for a living.

This fellow took me to the showroom floor where there were racks and racks of suits. Thousands of them. He said, "Pick out anything you want. I'll take care of it." So I chose a dark blue suit and he picked up the tab. Don't know what a suit cost at that time. I'm sure he bought it wholesale. Maybe he talked to the owner of the factory about me and got a break. The first time I put on the suit, I was on my way to temple in Winthrop. It was a Saturday. Uncle Harry asked, "Where did you get that suit?" I told him I met this friend of Jack's. That I went to the factory and watched him cut fabric. And he took me to the warehouse and said pick out anything you want. Uncle Harry had no response.

I don't think Jack pitched in on the suit, because he was tight with a dollar. Jack was the type of guy that made me pay the driving toll for the tunnel if I wanted to spend the night in Winthrop instead of going back to Dorchester. I'd pay while I was in the car and when he was driving back, he'd pay himself. Sometimes we'd go on a date and he'd look at the bill and figure out to the penny what it cost. If I didn't have any money, he'd write out a slip of paper. Leon owes me. He was that type of fellow. In one way, he was very generous. In the other way, he felt I should get used to paying. Bottom line was he'd never pick up the tab, even though he had plenty of money. At the end of each week, first thing he did was buy a U.S. bond and put it away. He lived at home with his father, so certainly he didn't have too much expense. Except for the car.

I'd been in America for seven or eight months. My visa was going to expire in a month or two. I began to get serious about immigration. In the beginning, Morris the lawyer expressed an interest in me. But soon enough, he came around to Uncle's Harry way of thinking. I knew this because he was no longer cooperative. I'd stop by the office he shared with some other lawyers near the factory. He'd be too busy to give me attention. Morris worked nights at a post office. Even though he came out of Harvard Law School, his day position was a secondary job for him.

Besides working with Morris, I began to pursue other avenues for immigration. One of the things discussed was marrying an American citizen. Marriage didn't guarantee that I could stay, but it opened some doors. Once this became knowledge, Jack introduced me to a woman that served in the United States Army. She was a couple years older than me. Jack thought maybe this could be a *shiddach*. An arranged marriage. A get-together with somebody that might help me obtain citizenship. Jack knew her family and thought she'd be willing to participate. So at least I'd have papers. One or two meetings I had with her one-to-one. It was discussed on a professional basis, but I wasn't interested in her. I didn't want just any wife. She had to be somebody I loved.

By now I was getting pressured by the Israeli government to come back and serve in the reserves. I got notices on a monthly basis through the Israeli consulate. And I was threatened with penalties if I didn't show up. But I ignored them. I thought, "Look, I'll pay my penalties when I get there." After all, I was here, they were there. What could they do to me? The INS, the Immigration and Naturalization Service, sent letters advising me that my visa was going to expire and I should take action. I wasn't taking their notices that seriously either. The blind lawyer I met through Morris told me I ought to go for a short time to Haiti. Because it was so close to the United States. Or go to Cuba and spend some time there. It was easier to come in through those countries than coming back from Israel. Those were options but they didn't work for me. I had no connections in those countries.

Learning a Trade

One thing I decided to do was learn a trade or a skill. Even if I had to go back to Israel, I wanted to go back with some tools or training. There I was working for American Kosher, sweeping floors and packaging salami. Not learning a thing. So at the end of 1951, I applied to Massachusetts Trade School on High Street in Boston. The one enrollment requirement was passing a math test, which I did. And I was accepted for a three-month course. I figured I could use that program as a way to get another extension on my visa. There was only one problem. The tuition. A lump sum of 250 bucks. Going to Uncle Harry and asking money for school wasn't going to happen, because he wasn't for that. He'd say, "Why are you going to waste your time? If you want a trade, why don't you learn my business? I'll send you to some courses. Learning my business would be a lot more profitable than your training program." That was his philosophy. He wasn't going to pay for something he didn't approve of.

I had long discussions with Jack about how I was going to find money for trade school. We'd be on the phone talking forever. Or we'd pull off at the side of a street in Dorchester and sit in the car and talk all night. Many times the police went back and forth in their cruisers. They kept an eye on us. They saw these two guys sitting in the car in the middle of the night. They saw us at 2:00 a.m. Then at 3:00 a.m. They'd knock on the window and ask what we were doing. Jack would say, "I live here and this is my friend who lives in Winthrop. We get together occasionally and talk." And then the officer would ask him for his license. Just to make sure that's where he lived. They never asked for my license because I was his friend. But the officer would say, "Don't you think it's about time you got in the house?" No, we'd sit until 4:00 in the morning and then go to bed and sleep for an hour.

After a few days of talking, Jack said, "I'll lend you the money. You'll pay me back some day." I told him, "Jack, I'm not going to do that." We decided I would ask the school if they'd give me a loan or a scholarship. The next day I met with the admissions lady. I told her, "I don't have the money. Could I possibly get some financial assistance?" She asked me on what grounds and I explained myself. Evidently, it hit a nerve and she took me up to the president, Mr. Gouse. He was Jewish, a very kind man. He told me he'd give me an informal loan. He said, "We're not going to sign any papers. I'll leave it up to you to pay it back."

I started the program and was trained to be a draftsman. It was a two-part course. One part was drafting and the other part was machining. They taught students how things were made after directions were drawn. I learned algebra, geometry and trigonometry. It was a beneficial course and I passed with all flying colors. I even got a diploma from Massachusetts Trade School. It could be used anyplace I applied for a job. After passing the course, I wanted to get more training. To help me further. So I used my trade school diploma and got a scholarship to a night program at Wentworth Technical Institute. I attended the program a couple of weeks but the logistics were complicated. Had no means of getting there from Winthrop. I went a couple of nights straight from the factory. But working for Uncle Harry all day and then going to Wentworth at night was too much of a hassle. I dropped out of the program.

After that, I enrolled in an Associates Degree program at Northeastern, again at night. A two-year engineering program. I showed them my diploma and was accepted. I didn't complete that program either, but I worked hard. I was beginning to acquire tools. I could knock on a door and say I could do some drawings. Or I could run a piece of equipment. Finally, I had some options. All of this training not only gave me skills. It helped me get extensions on my visa. By showing a piece of paper that I was accepted for a certain program, I was able to stay in the United States for two years. I got three or four extensions in six-month intervals. Keep in mind, the whole time I was going to training programs, I worked for Uncle Harry. Made time for it. I had to follow a schedule for him but I wasn't punching a card. It was a matter of yes, I put in the hours because he provided me room and board. I never asked to get paid.

Dating

Back then, I had what was called a little black book. In it were close to 150 names of girls. Some of them one shot deals. Some of them longer. But nothing had clicked. I dated one girl from Winthrop a few times. She was a show-off who had to have the upper hand on things. A small pin bowler. Practically lived in the bowling alley. I never bowled in my life. That didn't fly with me.

Another girl I met through a guy that owned a deli in Lowell. This guy would call up an order at American Kosher and I'd make the delivery. One day, he invited his niece to the deli because he knew I was coming with an order. She was a pretty girl, about my age. Her father owned an automobile agency, and she drove her own Caddy. I was intrigued. She took a liking to me and I dated her a bunch of times. She used to drive all the way from Lowell to Winthrop to see me because I didn't have a car. Each time she'd show up with a different vehicle and let me drive. Oh, the cars she showed up with. Cadillacs. Convertibles. I was really impressed. Then she invited me over her house. She picked me up on a Sunday and we drove back to Lowell. It was a fancy place but I didn't like the family. That visit killed the relationship. She called and showed up a couple more times. I told her we were wasting time. Didn't want to pursue it. After that, I dated an Israeli girl who spoke Hebrew. She lived in Dorchester but I wasn't interested in her. So she introduced me to a friend of hers. I dated that girl a couple times but nothing came of it.

My life was moving on pretty good in this country. I was going to school, having a social life. Continuously going to dances. At one of those dances, I met Estelle Bornstein. It was at the Bradford Hotel on a Saturday night and I was with Jack. I noticed Edith, Estelle's sister, on the dance floor. She looked a woman of my age. I was twenty-three at that time. I went up and I asked if I could have the next dance. When you dance, you talk. She told me she was twenty-four years old and going through a divorce with Harold, her husband of three years. After the dance, she rebuffed me. I had a feeling it was because of my accent. But she thought I wasn't a bad looking guy. Maybe her sister Estelle could be fixed up with a fellow like me. So she introduced me to Estelle. She was twenty years old. I didn't ask her to dance but she stuck in my mind. I met quite a few girls that night. After the evening was over, I took the subway back to Winthrop.

The funny thing was that I had met Edith's husband, Harold, before I met the Bornstein sisters. But I didn't put two and two together that night. Harold worked at Arthur Flooring on Blue Hill Avenue in Dorchester, near Jack's house. One day, Jack and I were across the street from the store and Harold was standing outside. We walked by and started a conversation. Harold was separated from Edith by then. We got to be friendly and after a while Harold and I went on a double date at the Music Hall. The plan was dinner after the movies with two girls from Brookline. Their names came from my little black book. I didn't know it, but Harold already knew these girls. And for some reason, he didn't like them.

As soon as we picked him up, he thought of a dodge. We came into the theater, and I was a gentleman so I guided the girls to their seats. Harold excused himself and left. Walked right out the front door of the theater. Well, the tickets were paid for. It didn't take long for the girls to realize he was gone. After the movie, I apologized. I wasn't going to take two girls out to dinner. Drove them home. Soon after, I went to the store to find Harold. I said, "What the hell did you do that for? What kind of person are you?" I let him have it. So when I met Edith at the dance, it was a strange coincidence that I already knew her husband.

After the dance, a few weeks went by. Jack was helping to organize a party in Dorchester for a Friday night. A girl named Judy was in charge of finding girls for the party and Jack was supposed to bring boys. He stopped by the factory a few days before the party and we talked about who was coming. He asked if we should invite Estelle Bornstein. I still had her telephone number in Dorchester. We agreed and Jack asked Judy to give her a call. I came with Judy to pick her up in Uncle Harry's Pontiac. Uncle Harry didn't mind me driving his car. Thought I was a better driver than anybody in the family. We climbed up two flights of stairs and Estelle was in curlers, getting fixed up. We waited in the hallway ten, fifteen minutes. She finally came out. And she looked lovely. The party was a couple streets from Estelle's house. I bumped into a little blonde girl I met before. I talked a bit with Estelle, but most of the time I spent with other girls.

Then came a situation where I needed a date. Jack and I were going to double date and he already chose his girl. Jack recommended the girl I picked up in Dorchester. The one whose sister I danced with. Estelle Bornstein. It was a Friday night and I couldn't make the call because nobody used the phone at Uncle Harry's house on Shabbat. The date was for Saturday, the next day. Really short notice. At that time, few girls would go on a date at such short notice. It was like they were announcing that some guy came in and saved them so they wouldn't have to spend Saturday night, which was a big night, at home by themselves. Anyway, Jack made the call. Gave Estelle a story that Leon Rubinstein was at his uncle's place and it was a religious house. That I planned to call earlier during the week but I couldn't. Because I was tied up at work and school. And she agreed to go out.

Saturday night, we drove up in Jack's car. I already knew the house because I'd been there before. Estelle was ready that time. We went to the first 3D movie that came to the Music Hall in Boston. *The House of Wax* with Vincent Price. At the movies, they handed out 3D stereoscopic glasses made of cardboard. Now, Estelle wore prescription glasses. Contact lenses were not available at that time. She tried to hold the 3D glasses on top of her own glasses but they didn't fit comfortably. So she was holding the cardboard glasses and fidgeting with them. And I was unhappy because I couldn't hold her hand. She was so busy fussing with the glasses that I couldn't make contact. I wanted to put my arms around her and be intimate. Touch her. Maybe give her a little kiss on the neck. I was a romantic guy. And God knows she was a very appealing person. But how could I be close to a girl that was so involved with her hands, with the glasses, and concentrating on the movie?

Finally I said to her, "Show me the glasses and I'll fix them so you won't be tying up your hands with them." She took off her eyeglasses and handed them to me. I took the 3D glasses and made a slit on each side with my fingernail. And I slid them right over her eyeglasses. Well, Estelle thought that was just magical. She thought I was really clever. There we were smiling at each other. And I finally got to hold her hand. After all that. And her hands were freezing. When the movie ended, we got to keep those 3D glasses as a memento. We went to Jack and Marion's on Harvard Street in Brookline and had New York cheesecake and coffee. After that date, I started to call her on a weekly basis.

Estelle was working in Boston for the Jewish Big Brother Association and we'd meet for lunch. I'd go to this little luncheonette around the corner from American Kosher and pick up a couple of big bulky rolls. The rolls only cost three cents, maybe five cents apiece, but the owner and his wife liked me and gave them to me for free. I'd take the rolls to the factory and slice up two pounds of corned beef. Put one pound on each bulky. Since most of the guys ate their lunch at the factory, there was always a jar of mustard available to break up the monotony of the meat. So I spread a little mustard on the bulkies for flavor. On my way to see Estelle, I'd pick up a few half sour pickles at a deli I knew. Without paying a dime. This was all for nothing.

I'd meet her with these corned beef sandwiches wrapped in white paper. One of them was enough for an army. She never saw anything like it. She realized, "Gee, this isn't so bad." We'd sit on a bench at Park Square or Boston Common and have lunch and talk, enjoying each other's company. Then she'd rush back to the office. Soon I was seeing her on the average of four times a week, at least. Almost every weekend we were going out and sometimes at night during the week. Not elaborate dates. Never took her out to dinner. But we used to go for lunch. And brunch on Boylston Street. It wasn't always a sandwich.

After six weeks, I began talking to Estelle about getting married. I mentioned it one Friday night to Uncle Harry and Aunt Alice and they went bananas. "Why do you want to do this? You hardly know this girl!" Believe me, there was some spark because they knew I was serious. They had already met Estelle since I brought her to Winthrop on a Sunday and introduced them. When I told them I wanted to marry her, they didn't want to hear about it. They might have talked to Bob Levine's father, Hymie, about Estelle's family. Because he knew everything and he had their ear. Evidently there was nothing pleasant said about this particular family that I was interested in. I don't know what they talked about. But people gossip.

At that point, Uncle Harry became completely focused on me returning to Israel. All the talk was concentrated on me going back. Forget about the engagement. Forget about marriage. I told him I wouldn't listen. I wouldn't have anything to do with it. Then he said, "I'll give you two thousand dollars if you get on that plane. And that's besides the ticket. You'll have some money to buy a business in Israel." Two thousand dollars in those days was like $200,000 today. I really could have bought something. But not a business in Israel. The big businesses were all government-owned. Anyway, I would have none of that. I said to him, "Money's not an issue. I can always make money. I want to stay here and marry Estelle." A few days later, we were headed into the factory. I was driving the car and he told me to think seriously about the offer he made. Because it wasn't going to be dragged out. The offer was a one-shot deal. And I said to him, "I don't want your $2,000." So he said, "How about $3,000? Will that do the job?" I said to him, "No, that's not going to work."

Uncle Harry kept bringing up Dr. Lubrani during our discussions. That Dr. Lubrani could help me start a business in Israel. Dr. Lubrani's son, Uri, was the man I used to chauffeur from Tel Aviv to Haifa when I was in the military. His father was also a prominent, influential person in Israel. I corresponded with Uri while I was in Winthrop, and in 1953, his father wrote to say he was coming to New York via London. Looking for a publisher for a children's book he wrote. He had a weekend stop over in Boston and asked if he could stay with me and my family because he didn't want to register at a hotel. Uncle Harry agreed. I picked him up at Logan Airport and brought him to Winthrop.

Dr. Lubrani soon learned that Uncle Harry was in the meat business and had his own factory. Part of Dr. Lubrani's function in Israel was running the department that sent out inspectors to butcheries. To make sure sanitation rules were observed. I don't think there were too many rules because in those days, you'd walk into a butchery to buy a chicken or a pound of beef and walk out with it wrapped in a newspaper. They didn't have the special type of wax papers we used at American Kosher. Anyway, Uncle Harry was impressed with Dr. Lubrani. So when Uncle Harry was offering me money, he said, "You have strong connections like Dr. Lubrani. He could help you get going with a business." He said I should use Lubrani's expertise, his talent. Well, that wasn't something I was thinking about.

Once I announced my intentions to marry Estelle, Aunt Alice asked me about a wedding ring. She knew I'd set my mind on marriage. She said, "I'll take you to my jeweler. And we'll buy a ring." Uncle Harry wasn't there. We went to see Joe Gann, the jeweler. He and Aunt Alice knew each other well. He told me, "Pick any ring and the price will be the same." We came up with a combination engagement and marriage ring for Estelle. And then I picked out a ring for myself with yellow and white gold. Wasn't a plain round ring. On the white gold, it had some flats in it. I had a flavor for these things. He put the rings in small, velvet boxes and Aunt Alice paid $75 for them. Uncle Harry had nothing to do with it.

After the purchase, Aunt Alice decided we should go out to lunch with Estelle. Now, when Aunt Alice went out for lunch, she had a tuna sandwich. Something kosher. And I was used to easting kosher so I'd order a tuna sandwich, too. But not Estelle. She said, "I'll have a BLT on toast." A bacon, lettuce and tomato sandwich. On toast. I didn't know what a BLT was. But I knew that toast was something people didn't usually order. Because toast was done with butter on a side plate. When Aunt Alice heard BLT, she was really taken aback. Well, I didn't stop that sandwich from coming to the table. I'd never heard of this BLT. Even though I was in the country for two years. The people I went out with, they never ordered a BLT. If I knew what it was, I would have told her, "Send this back." Because I didn't eat bacon. I knew better.

You can imagine how that went over in Winthrop. When I came home, that was the discussion at the table. Nothing else was important. We were eating kosher food but talking BLTs. Uncle Harry bawled me out. "You realize what you're getting into?" I said to him, "Believe me, it's not going to happen again. This is not the type of home I'm going to have." Well, I heard about the BLT until after my wedding. That thing never got away. Even years later, after I established myself and had kids, Uncle Harry never forgot the BLT.

Soon after that, I proposed to Estelle. Over lunch one windy day at Boston Common. That's where I showed her the ring. In fact, the ring was given over with a sandwich. Apparently, she was thinking about it and was going to tell me, "No. I can't." That our courtship was too quick. She was ready to tell me it was all off. But I was persuasive. Had so much charisma. And I won her over.

When Estelle told her boss at Jewish Big Brother about the proposal, he said, "If you were my daughter, a beautiful girl like you, what are you doing with a guy without a family? I would never let you marry him." But you know, Estelle cared for me. She thought I was special. Honest. Generous. And I was crazy about her. She was the nicest girl I ever met. The best-looking girl I ever met. She was smart, mature. And I wanted to marry her. I didn't view her as a means of staying in the country. Didn't think it through, to be honest. I didn't realize how serious a commitment it would be. Nobody talked about the responsibilities of marriage back then.

After Estelle accepted my proposal, I ran the whole way back to the factory. Happy all over. Aunt Alice was there because it was the day she came in to do the books. I told her in Yiddish about the proposal. Explained how it happened. She wasn't too enthusiastic about it. She was matter-of-fact. "You said it would happen, it happened." She asked me whether Estelle liked the ring. Of course, I told her she loved it.

Estelle and I started planning the wedding but Uncle Harry wasn't going to pay for any part of it. Usually, the groom's family provides the music and the bar. Well, music was not to be. And the bar was not to be. Estelle's family didn't have much money, but they were prepared to pay for the whole wedding. Needless to say, it was a subdued atmosphere in the house in Winthrop. Uncle Harry made me an offer for $3,000 to leave the country and I wouldn't accept it. It was a large sum they were willing to part with, in order to part with me, too. On the other hand, maybe they felt it was a small amount to get me out of there. Maybe they were thinking $5,000 would have made me leave. I never would have accepted any amount of money. It wasn't my goal to go back to Israel and start a business. If I had asked him, "What type of business do you think I could start in Israel with $2,000?" He would have answered, "How about a sausage factory?"

Newlyweds

Estelle knew about my immigration status before we married. I'd discussed everything with her while we were dating. That I was an Israeli citizen and owed the Israeli government time for the reserves. At some point, I needed to return and complete my military duty. It was a matter of serving one month each year. In my case, I had to give them three months. Peacetime service. I knew if everything worked out, the Israeli government would let me return to America. Wasn't like they were putting me in jail. But no matter what, Estelle wasn't coming with me to Israel. We didn't have the capital. And what would I do with her there? I had no place for her to stay. On my own I could handle it. But with Estelle, it would be difficult.

I asked Estelle, "Do I take care of my military obligations right away or do I establish myself in Boston first?" It was pay me now or pay me later. Estelle and I decided I'd serve my three months in the reserves following our wedding. Get it over with. Then I'd return to the States, look for a job, get us settled in our own apartment. Uncle Harry wasn't involved with my decision. But I still maintained a good relationship. I told him and Aunt Alice, "I'm staying in this country and I want to have good relations with you. You're the only relatives I have."

Estelle and I were married on May 24, 1953 in Roxbury, Massachusetts. It was a dim, closed temple and we were married by Lenny Small, Ruth's husband. His first wedding as a rabbi. Mostly family showed up. Aunt Shancy, Uncle Harry, Aunt Alice, my cousins, Estelle's relatives. A couple of friends. Jack and Arthur in their fancy suits. Estelle's father took out a bottle of Canadian Club and poured a shot of whiskey to make a toast. Arthur took some photographs. Wasn't much of a wedding, but we got some money as gifts. One of Estelle's cousins gave us $300. They lived in Newton and had a cleaning store in Wellesley. In those days, $300 was a lot of money. Other people gave $25. Some guests didn't dish out any money at all.

I went to Uncle Harry with the envelopes of gift money and told him, "Open up an account for me and put the money in the bank." I'm not sure he ever did. He used some of the money to buy me a one-way ticket to Israel. The rest of that money never came back. Estelle was upset with me that I entrusted Uncle Harry with the money instead of her father. But I only met Estelle's father and mother one time before our wedding. When I picked her up to take her to the party. After that, I was never at her house. I saw her family at our wedding.

The first night of our marriage we spent in a small hotel in Kenmore Square in Boston. The next morning, we headed off on our honeymoon. A resort in the Catskills called the Laurels. We took a bus from Boston and changed buses in New York State. We spent a week at the Laurels getting to know each other. The weather was gorgeous. Hot sunny days, warm summer nights. Plenty of activities. Lots of food. Every morning, I'd jump into a rowboat before Estelle got up for breakfast. I'd row for half an hour and work up an appetite. God knows, I had quite an appetite. At the end of the week, we made the trip in reverse and returned to Boston. Jack picked us up at the bus station.

Before our honeymoon, I had made arrangements for us to stay with Bob Levine's father, Hymie, when we returned. He had a three-bedroom apartment in Dorchester. The first floor of a three decker. Hymie's wife had passed away by an accident a few months earlier, in February of 1953. It happened at home. Something was wrong with the boiler and the heat didn't come on. In those days, they had a cast iron boiler powered by coal. Bob's mother went down that morning to feed the boiler and it exploded. She was burned to death. Hymie was living on his own, grieving for his wife. By then, his son Bob was married and had his own apartment nearby.

We stayed with Hymie for less than a week. He got tired of us. Our routine didn't jive with him. In the mornings, Estelle went to her job and I went to American Kosher. Every day, we met for lunch in Boston. In the afternoon, I went to school. We came home and made dinner with meat I brought from American Kosher. We were clean, well behaved. Not party type of people. We didn't bring any juke boxes or radios. Just the clothes on our backs. After a few days, Hymie told us to leave. We went to stay with Estelle's parents, but that didn't last long because her sister objected. Not enough room in the house. The situation was not in my favor. I didn't have money for an apartment. Remember, Uncle Harry wasn't paying me. We decided it was time for me to return to Israel. Estelle would live with her parents until I returned.

I left the United States on June 13th, two weeks after we got married. My visa had been extended through the summer, so I left the country legally with the proper papers. I arrived in Haifa on June 28th and stayed with Ezra that night. Next morning, I reported to the reserves. I was stationed in a military base north of Haifa. They showed me the kitchen where I'd eat my meals, gave me a cot in the barracks. My second day, I visited the American consulate to start the paperwork to return to Estelle. I knew I'd need a new passport and visa. I'd brought documentation with me. The marriage license, Estelle's birth certificate. The paperwork was bound to be a slow process.

Back in Israel

In the reserves, I was among strange people. Nobody I knew from before. But I was social, met some nice fellows. A couple of them had high rank. I was assigned to an artillery unit as the driver. My position changed from time to time. It depended on where I was needed. Most of the time we were on maneuvers. Driving at night, moving from place to place. Establishing camps.

On Saturdays, I was off. Most of the guys went home to their families. I usually went to Yagur to see Aharon. He was still working in the office. Had quite a few girlfriends. Some Saturdays, I'd show up and he'd say, "Come with me." He had distant relatives that lived in the suburbs of Haifa. We'd take a bus and visit them. Get some family time. A couple of afternoons we visited a cousin of his who wanted to take a trip to the United States. A married woman without children. Aharon wanted me to talk with her about America. After all, I was from there now. So we got together, had a meal. Told her about life in the United States.

I was lonely. Missed Estelle terribly. But I tried to keep busy. On a weeknight or a weekend, there'd be hundreds of people hanging around the cinema in Haifa. I'd go there to bump into the crowd, look for faces I might recognize. Stuck my hands in my pockets, walked around. Didn't have money for the movies but it was a chance to socialize. Ezra was still working like a slave, driving the cab at night and occasionally hauling bleach with his brother. I'd see him now and then. I visited the tailor that fixed my blue suit. Unannounced, I'd knock on the door. His wife would let me in, give me a meal. Spent a couple of Saturdays with guys I met in the reserves. And I reconnected with soldiers I served with previously.

One soldier I visited, his mother made a remark. How come I showed up empty-handed, without bringing a gift? Here I was supposed to be wealthy, living in America. But most of the guys I visited gave me a warm reception. We're talking about soldiers working side-by-side, day after day. Some very close ties were established. When I saw them, they wanted to know what I was doing, how I was. I showed them photographs of Estelle, pictures from our wedding. A few times I went out with a girl I dated in Boston, who came to live with her sister in Haifa. Nothing romantic, of course. Just a chance to have some female companionship.

Estelle was writing me letters on a daily basis. There wasn't a day when I wouldn't get two or three letters. All on the same stationary. The thin paper that's folded in three parts. She used to buy it by the hundreds at the post office. Those letters came to Ezra. When he'd see me, he'd bring a pack of them. I wrote back once a week.

A lot of changes happened in Haifa during the two years I was gone. When I left in '51, there were no traffic lights at intersections. When I came back in '53, the first traffic light was installed. I was accustomed to traffic lights in the United States, but most people in Haifa never saw anything like it. They put one light at a dangerous intersection at the bottom of the Carmel. Driving down that hill, people couldn't stop even if they wanted to. Everyone would sit by the intersection and watch the light switch from green to red. There were other changes, too. Jobs were available. There was more commerce. Money poured in. Foreign companies appeared and did work that was needed after the War of Independence. Not because of destruction, because of deterioration.

Funny thing. While I was in the reserves, I visited Dr. Lubrani and mentioned Uncle Harry's business idea. That he was planning to give me a chunk of money to start a factory in Israel. Dr. Lubrani wasn't receptive at all. He said, "You're dreaming if you think you can come here and start a business like that. It takes a lot of money. It takes a lot of guts to make it happen." There were quite a few small businesses in Israel at that time. Not big businesses. If you ran a butcher shop and certain meats didn't sell, you'd make it into a product. Maybe a sausage or salami. So there was that type of business. But very few people came and set up a factory in Israel in those days. Not unless it was government subsidized.

By the end of September, I finished my time in the reserves. Gave them the three months. There weren't any penalties and everything went smoothly. The government issued me a document stating my time was served honorably. I was always in the best of behavior. Minded my own business and did what I was told. Never fought the system.

While I was waiting on my passport and visa, I found a shared room to rent not far from the consulate in Haifa. Walking distance, about five blocks. The room was in a four-story apartment building. Because of the shape of the land, two floors were below street level and two floors were above. It was a small, sunny room on the second floor. Had a beautiful view overlooking the lower part of the city and the port of Haifa. Came with a bed and linens. Most of the renters in that building were young professionals who didn't have their own furniture.

I shared the room with Shlomo, a driving instructor. A good friend of Ezra's. He owned a vehicle that was used as a cab at night. During the daytime, he had a license to teach drivers. He took me in because he couldn't handle the rent on his own. But there was one rule. No food in the room. In Israel, like any tropical place, there's trouble with bugs. They didn't want anyone eating inside. So I ate outdoors, usually one meal a day. I lost a lot of weight that year. First, I got skinny in the military. Then only one meal a day. It wasn't too bad, though, because I knew it was a temporary situation.

I had no trouble getting a job while the consulate was working on my documents. This time, there was an abundance of work. At first, I worked for a small machine shop in Haifa. The guy had a backlog of hundreds and hundreds of electric motors. My job was to clean up the motors. The owner would fix them up and sell them. The biggest problem with these motors was the carbon brushes not having the proper spring loads, and they would wear out. I'd take an armature, the central part of the motor, put it on an old Italian lathe, and clean it up nice. Make sure it didn't have any rough spots. It involved cutting carbon with a hacksaw. Primitive work.

After that, I got a job at a Swedish company that was renovating the one big flour mill in Haifa. It was an old plant, built in the late 1800s or early 1900s. And they modernized it. Put in large electric motors to drive the machines that ground the wheat. It was a huge undertaking and they did it in stages. They had quite a task on their hands, this Swedish company. My job was making keys for different shafts. The keys fit in the shafts to support the belt driven wheels that came from the motor. Again, primitive work. I was given a steel rod and cut it with a hacksaw. Squared it off. The keys were heated at high temperatures and dropped in a vat of oil for hardening. I did this for couple of weeks and got bored.

Then I went to work for two friendly young fellows who were welders. They fixed the machines for companies that specialized in grinding rocks into pebbles. And they had a good amount of work as well. One of the jobs they landed was for a Jewish businessman from Europe who took over a building outside of Haifa. Through some connections under the table, he set up a paint factory. Brought in machines from overseas. I did assembly work on these machines for a few weeks. The paint factory guy had other jobs he wanted me to go on. But they were too dangerous. One job he offered was helping to build a bridge over a busy highway. This was for a company taking stone off of Mount Carmel and moving it to the other side of the road. The bridge for the conveyer belt was sixteen or twenty feet high. I said, "Sorry, I'm afraid of heights. I'll go find myself something else."

Around that time, Ezra got a job transporting fiberglass sheeting from Haifa to the Negev, where former Prime Minister Ben-Gurion was building a house. Ezra needed a driver and asked me whether I'd take the job. Back then, the Negev was the wilderness and it was dangerous to drive. There were still skirmishes going on, especially in the open spaces. I didn't know the destination exactly, but I knew it was after Mashabei

Sadeh, the kibbutz where my friends were. There was only one road, so I couldn't get lost. It wasn't a good quality road, though. Ezra said to me, "You want to do it or not? I have the truck. I have the job. But it's not paying much." I said to myself, "I have nothing else to do. I'll take the job and deliver the fiberglass. Plus I'll visit my friends at Mashabei Sadeh." I got up at four o'clock in the morning and drove to the port because the fiberglass sheeting came in from Europe by ship. The port workers were unionized in those days and they loaded the truck for me. All I had to do was unload it when I got to my destination. I drove straight to the Negev and delivered the fiberglass. I saw the two-bedroom house that was being built for Ben-Gurion.

When I left Israel in 1951, Ben-Gurion was the Prime Minister. When I came back, he'd given up the post and was running a campaign to encourage young people to move to open spaces rather than living in congested places like Tel Aviv. Few people wanted to leave the safety of the city. Ben-Gurion took his wife to the desert to show that it was possible. And now they were building this nice house with fiberglass insulation for the former Prime Minister. Most of the people that lived there never had insulation.

I finished the job and drove to Mashabei Sadeh. My friends in the kibbutz, I hadn't seen them in two years. I stepped down from the truck and heard someone call my name. Soon a crowd gathered around. The hugs, the kisses, slaps on the back. The reception was unbelievable. The guy cleaning the barn stopped what he was doing and took time to see me. The girls collecting eggs in the chicken coop put down their work. It wasn't a big place. I stayed a couple of hours. Then I had to get back to Haifa. On the drive, I thought about how far we'd come. There was a time when there was some jealousy. That I'd left a place where I was needed and went to the United States for luxury. Those pioneers at the kibbutz were dedicated. Hardworking. What I did was looked down on. But that didn't last long. After all, they were my brothers and sisters. My family of orphans.

When I returned from Mashabei Sadeh, I decided to try the American embassy in Tel Aviv. I was getting no results as far as my paperwork in Haifa. By this time, six or seven months had gone by since I completed my military duty and I was still no closer to getting back to Estelle. Several times, Estelle approached Uncle Harry to get help with the consulate in America but he wasn't responsive. Here I was, a married man trying to get back to my wife. Couldn't get either consulate to budge. Estelle and I continued to correspond. Never lost faith we'd be reunited. But Estelle was so upset that she stopped getting her period. At the Tel Aviv embassy, I asked to speak to a supervisor. My English was pretty good, even though I was speaking mostly Hebrew at that time. A supervisor named Mr. Parker met with me. Tall, handsome guy in his forties. He was gay. Wasn't hard figuring that out. He listened to my story, very attentive. I could tell he liked my looks. He said, "Come back in the morning and I'll see what I can do."

By then it was afternoon and I decided to stop by my friend Kalman's place in Peta Tikva, just outside of Tel Aviv. See if I could stay there overnight. Kalman was still in the service, a high ranking officer in the paratroopers. I got there late in the day and knocked on the door. His house was built of chicken coop and crates from grapefruits. Falling apart. Kalman's in-laws answered the door but didn't understand me. They were Arab Jews from Iraq and spoke little Hebrew. Kalman's wife Sarah worked during the day so they called in her older sister. I was told to wait. I sat on a crate and looked around. Sarah's mother and father slept on one side of the room. Kalman and Sarah had a bed in another corner. The only thing separating them was a blanket. They had a small gas stove. And outside, a little orchard of grapefruit trees.

Soon Sarah came home but she didn't know a thing about me. Even though I corresponded with Kalman once a month. I never told him about the food I ate and the house I lived in. The friends I had. So different from his life. Sarah didn't prepare any food because Kalman ate his meals at the base. She and I talked for a while and then Kalman walked in. Gave me a bear hug. Asked how I was doing. Told me to stay with them for a few days. Still the same Kalman from the orphanage in Bytom, looking out for me. We talked until late at night, the way old friends do. I slept on the floor.

The next morning, I went to see Mr. Parker at the embassy. Filled out forms, showed my documents. He shuffled papers on his desk and told me to come back the next day. And the day after, and the day after that. He took an interest in me. One night, he invited me to his house. We drank whiskey and talked about America. The following Saturday, Mr. Parker brought me to the home of an Indian couple who worked for the Indian embassy. He introduced me as a friend. They served a traditional Indian meal and the food was so very spicy. Everything I touched. Hot and spicy. Plenty of beer and wine to wash it down. Picture it on a hot day. Spicy food. The extra wine I wasn't used to.

It was late when we left and I was tipsy. I decided to take a bus to Bella's house. She was a girl from Yagur who married a contractor. If I showed up, she'd take me in for the night. But somehow I wound up in Mr. Parker's place. He gave me my own bed, but he made several advances. And I couldn't handle it. I told him to cool it. Didn't mean to give him the wrong impression. I was a married man. Finally, I said, "Mr.

Parker, I don't want to be put in a position where I have to report you." Needless to say, that was the wrong thing to tell him. I needed the guy. He had an in at the embassy. Somebody of stature. He was my salvation with the paperwork. I tried to persuade him this was not the right thing to do.

In the middle of the night, I left. The buses weren't running. I walked fifteen miles to Bella's house. Started my walk at three a.m. and made it to her place by midmorning. I showed up like nothing happened. Her husband was at work. She was home with her daughter, thrilled to see me. Made me breakfast and I took a nap. I left there in the afternoon. Couldn't bear to go back to the embassy.

But eventually, I did go back. I was tired of waiting. Anxious to see Estelle. Within a week, I returned to the embassy and talked to Mr. Parker again. He was polite and helped me with the paperwork. Never mentioned what happened between us.

For months, I'd been corresponding with Uncle Harry and begging him to serve as my sponsor. Without sponsorship, I couldn't enter America. The American government didn't want to bring in immigrants and have them stand in the unemployment line. America was at war with Korea. It was the McCarthy era. The Rosenberg spy case was cooking and the government wasn't receptive to foreigners. Especially Jewish ones. They frowned on people born in a communist country like Poland. At that time, Poland was controlled by Russia. And that was a problem.

The bottom line was Uncle Harry didn't want to sponsor me because he couldn't guarantee me a job. His business was collapsing. The Central Artery was being built and all the factories in the area were being displaced. He was down to one truck on the road. I promised him if he sponsored me, I'd get a job on my own. After all, I'd studied drafting and had experience operating equipment. I was familiar with the English measurement system as well as the metric system. I pleaded with him to help me return to my wife. Finally Uncle Harry relented. He sent a letter stating he would take responsibility for me. It didn't take long after that. Things began to fall in place.

When my sponsorship was approved, I began to breathe easier. But in my heart, I knew that once I left, it would be a long time before I'd return to Israel. One of the last social events I went to was Moshe Trosman's wedding in Ramat Gan. Moshe was a close friend of Aharon's from Yagur. Both from the same town in Poland. Aharon got hold of me and said, "Moshe Trosman is getting married tomorrow night. And I want you to come."

I said, " I wasn't invited. I don't have clothes."

"Clothes shmothes. You're coming."

So I showed up with Aharon at the wedding, at Moshe's mother's house. As soon as I walked in the door, I heard someone call my name. It was Israel Fuchs, my neighbor from Manasterskya Street. The blacksmith. Somehow he made it from Poland to Israel. He took my face in his hands and kissed me. Kept his arm around my shoulder the whole time. Israel's second wife from Koretz remembered me, too. So it turned out that Moshe's wedding was a reunion as well as a celebration. Moshe's mother had been preparing for weeks. Made all the food herself. Israeli salads, falafel, hummus, pita bread, sodas and orange juice. We toasted with sweet red wine. They gathered everyone for a family picture. A black and white photograph. And I was in it.

The wedding ended late at night and Israel insisted I go to his home in Gadera. We took the last bus from Ramat Gan. Israel and his wife lived in a small place. Had their own chicken coop, their own eggs. Self-sufficient. I spent the night and we talked. Israel was my father's age. He told me he survived the war by taking off into the forest. His older brother from Koretz also survived. He was still working as a blacksmith, on the railroad cars in Haifa. The next morning Israel's wife made a big breakfast with fresh eggs. He hugged me. Made me promise to write from America.

After my sponsorship was accepted, Uncle Harry sent me the ticket for the ship. Even though he gave me such grief about going to Israel, something made him change his mind about accepting my return. Maybe he realized that a married man needs to be with his wife. Maybe Aunt Alice had some influence. At any rate, he gave a helping hand. And I wasn't going to question it. Almost eleven months had passed since I left Estelle. I was in the reserves for three months, then eight months for my papers to get approved. Too long a time to be separated.

Finally the day came for me to leave. It was April 13, 1954. Ezra brought me to the dock in Haifa. It was chaotic and loud, completely disorganized. People were everywhere. And who shows up? The port authority guy that bought me shoes in 1951.

He pointed at me and said, "This man can't leave the country. He owes me money."

My hands started shaking. I couldn't believe what was happening.

The port officer asked, "How much money does he owe you?"

"Nine pounds."

Nine pounds was about two dollars in those days. But I'd already exchanged my money. And I couldn't afford to part with any American dollars. Ezra, he heard everything.

Ezra turned to me. "Don't worry. I'll take care of it."

The guy pointed at me again. "It has to be money from him."

The port officer realized the guy was a bastard. He said, "You'll get your money. Leave him alone."

When that guy bought me shoes in Haifa two years before, he didn't expect me to repay. He paid for the shoes in exchange for me helping him when I got to America. He wanted me to contact his relative in Dorchester. Which I did. His relative was a crazy man in his forties. Lost an eye in World War II and came to America as a refugee. Must have lived on welfare. When I met him, he took his glass eye out and opened up the inside of his socket. Enough to scare the hell out of anybody. He started yelling at me. How dare I knock on his door. Don't bother him about his relative in Israel. Slammed the door in my face. I sent the port authority guy a letter about what happened. Since nothing resulted, he felt empty-handed. He was desperate to leave Israel but didn't have other contacts in the United States. He was a single, hard-working guy with the same problems as everybody.

Later, Ezra told me he would bump into this guy on the streets of Haifa. And Ezra would ignore him. What kind of character would do this to a person? It was so difficult to get out of Israel. And there I was, ten feet from the ship.

Ezra paid the guy his nine pounds and we said our goodbyes. At last, I boarded the vessel. It was a small Italian ship that sailed from port to port, hugging the coast. It stopped at Cyprus, Greece, the Dardanelles, then Italy. Took five days just to get to Naples. Our first stop was six hours at Nicosia, Cyprus. I grabbed my passport and went running. No use sitting on the boat. From there we went to Athens, where a group of us ran three or four miles up to the ruins. Finally we made it to Naples, early in the morning. But the ship to New York wasn't leaving from Naples this time. It was departing from Genoa. And my train to Genoa wasn't leaving until that evening.

To kill the time, I walked over to the Hotel International, where I'd stayed in 1951. I was traveling light, with my old suitcase. Everything looked the same. The sailors by the hotel, the street vendors selling meats and cheeses, even the restaurant where I learned to eat spaghetti.

In those days, there was little information for visitors. Barely any printed material as to where to go and what to see. Even local maps weren't available because the tourist business hadn't taken off. But I'd heard about the island of Capri and decided to take a roundtrip ferry to see the waterfall there. A photographic spot. That night, I boarded an overnight train to Genoa. Stayed in Genoa for six days, waiting for the S.S. America. One of the largest ships that sailed from Europe to the United States at that time.

It was terrible weather the day the S.S. America set sail. Late in the afternoon we left Genoa. The ship stopped in the Azores to let one storm pass. Stayed there six or eight hours. Didn't get off the ship. At last we took off and that night there was another raging storm. Half of the stairs on one side of the ship were swept away. Not only did the stairs disappear in the sea. The rescue boats on hangers, they disappeared, too. All around me, passengers were throwing up. Children were crying. I stayed way below deck. The deeper I went, the less rocking there was. Because of the storm, we were diverted to Halifax. Stuck again for another six or eight hours. But at least we were able to disembark. Halifax was a lush place. Magnificent greenery on a hill. Through the rain, we could see it from the ocean. I climbed up to a fortress where the British had their fortifications. Felt good to be on land, even in the downpour.

Some people that had the means didn't get back on the boat. It takes a while to recoup from being seasick. The rest of us made it to New York in a day. Since it wasn't my first trip into New York Port Authority, I chatted with other passengers, telling them what to expect. I was a know-it-all. An old man from my experience.

After twenty-two days, I finally arrived in New York. It was May 3, 1954. I got off the boat and cleared customs. The first time my ship docked in New York, Ruth was waiting for me. This time, Estelle was there. My beautiful American wife. I saw her standing in the crowd, straining to see me. She looked radiant in her short hair and sweater, her pleated skirt and heels. We hugged and kissed, laughing and crying. Couldn't let go of each other. Arm in arm, we walked to the Taft Hotel on Seventh Avenue, where Estelle had paid for a room.

Home

Next morning, Estelle and I went to Grand Central Station and boarded a train to Boston. It was a Tuesday. As soon as I stepped in Boston, I called my former teachers to get help with finding a job. These were the ones who taught me drafting and how to run equipment. One of them lived in Arlington and one in Belmont. I took buses, then walked. The teacher from Arlington, he made some calls for me. By Thursday, I had a job at Forbes Lithograph, in the Irish part of Chelsea.

Forbes Lithograph was a large printing facility. Their main job was printing money coupons for overseas soldiers. One press worked twenty-four hours a day printing these coupons, seven days a week. The next biggest job they had was printing the yellow paper wrappers for Beechnut chewing gum. Every week, they loaded a railroad car full of those wrappers. I used to ask myself, "Who the hell eats this much gum?" Another thing they printed and folded were brightly colored candy boxes.

My first day of work, I was taken around the plant. It was a huge brick factory with three floors. Part of the building was restricted because of the military printing. In the production rooms, the presses were filthy. Layers and layers of multi-colored ink built up from so much use.

Leon Rubinstein, age 25, Roxbury, Massachusetts, 1955.

My job was to disassemble the presses to get them ready for cleaning. I kept that position for a month or two. I earned sixty-one dollars a week, hourly pay. And I took as much work as I could get. Overtime. Whatever was available. After that, I was promoted to assembling. Earned another dime an hour. My next job was modifying the press to do different tasks. That involved some creative thinking. The highest paying job at Forbes was for a person who understood the way the presses ran. If they broke down, to get them back on line. That I never achieved. It took years and years to work up to that position.

Estelle was doing secretarial work at the Charlestown Navy Yard. In the morning, we'd leave together and go on separate commutes. We didn't mind. At first we stayed with Estelle's parents. Just for a week. The two of us shared Estelle's single bed. It was so narrow that I wound up on the floor. Then we stayed with Jack's neighbor, Mrs. Lazarus. Her husband passed away and she gave us a room. Mrs. Lazarus was a woman with something missing in her head. Most of the night she'd lay on the floor listening to the refrigerator. I'd wake up in the morning and she'd be sleeping on the linoleum.

I'd say, "Mrs. Lazarus, what are you doing?"

She'd say, "I want to make sure this thing works. If it doesn't, I don't know what I'm going to do. I don't have the money to buy one."

The other thing she did was sit in the living room and look out the window. One window with lace drapes.

She'd say, "This was what my husband used to do."

Mrs. Lazarus loved us. But something was off about her and we wanted our own place. After a couple of weeks, we went to a realtor who showed us a second floor apartment on Maple Street in Roxbury. A living room, a bedroom and a kitchen. In the apartment next to us were two unmarried sisters. Back then we called them old maids. We took the apartment and they repainted it fresh for us. Sixty dollars a month rent. At last we had the money.

That same week, we went to the Blue Hill Credit Union and took out a thousand dollar loan. Got Estelle's father to co-sign. With the loan money, we bought a bedroom set and a kitchen table. A friend of Estelle's family was in the upholstery business. We got him to make up a couch and a boxy turquoise chair for the living room. The couch was charcoal with white spots. We always wanted the best. Every Wednesday night, we'd walk to Estelle's house and give her father money from my weekly paycheck. He'd stop by the credit union on his way home from work on Thursday and make the payments.

While Estelle and I were thriving, Uncle Harry was having a tough time with his business due to the Central Artery construction. He couldn't even provide work to Bob Levine, his own nephew. In fact, he set up a job for Bob with Colonial Provisions, one of his competitors, in the shipping department. The city provided space in South Boston for factories that were displaced but Uncle Harry didn't want to be part of that. Once his factory on John Street came down, he moved the business to Everett. Rented a building there. Soon after, Hymie Levine guided him to a building in Dorchester and Uncle Harry bought it. Bad decision. The neighborhood was deteriorating. Uncle Harry could have gone into a brick building in East Boston, but it was separated from

Boston by the Sumner Tunnel. And Uncle Harry didn't want to depend on the tunnel. A lot of his customers were north and west of Boston. So he settled on Dorchester. Well, it was a real drain. Eventually, he had to downsize the business into a small production.

Estelle and Jack were working hard to help me stay in America. I came back on an international student visa, good for one year. Jack insisted that I apply for American citizenship right away, which I did. I filled out papers and waited for my court date. In the meantime, Estelle met Julian Ansel, a state representative in Boston who wrote a letter on our behalf. And she networked with Ms. Alpert, a single woman in charge of the Hebrew Immigrant Aid Society in Boston. HIAS wasn't that effective assisting with citizenship. They did more with helping displaced Jews locate relatives. But Ms. Alpert gave us moral support.

My immigration status didn't affect my employment, and I stayed at Forbes Lithograph a little over a year. The only Jew in an Irish crowd but I was accepted. The oldest worker was seventy-five and the youngest was forty. I was the new kid on the block. Twenty-four years old. Every morning they gave me a friendly welcome. I felt good going to work. This Irish crowd knew how to enjoy life. They used to whoop it up. Especially in the alleys. There wasn't a month when somebody didn't pass away. Each time, there was a wake. I remember when one older Irish fellow passed. I put in a few hours of overtime and decided to go to his wake. There was a dancing party there. They were drinking. Eating hard-boiled eggs. They took the corpse out of the coffin. Danced with him. That's when I took off. I took the bus and the train home.

In the summer of 1954, I began looking for another job to make more money. I saw an ad in *The Boston Globe*. Tracer Labs on High Street was looking for a draftsman. I said to myself, "Maybe I could do that. It's closer than Chelsea." I called and scheduled an interview that afternoon. Mind you, the only business experience I had was my work at Forbes. But I was confident. I put on my dark blue suit and met with them. I was clean cut, I was smart. They were impressed with me. It was a match. They called up Mr. Alexi, a Russian who spoke quickly. After the Bolshevik Revolution, he fled to France as a child. Now he was a supervisor at Tracer Labs and spoke Russian, French and English. He had little training in the field but knew how to handle people. The fact that I came from Europe and spoke Russian, that helped. We exchanged a few words in his language.

Mr. Alexi briefly explained the projects at Tracer Labs. They were developing isotopes for x-ray equipment. They were also building equipment to detect radiation. And they were involved in secret projects for the military. He showed me the type of sensors they built. As big as an oversized pan. A light would go on or the color would change if the radiation level went up. Like a thermometer. Mr. Alexi asked if I understood what he was talking about. Somehow I knew exactly what they were doing. I never saw an isotope in my life. Never saw a measuring device for radiation. But I connected the dots. And I got the job.

Mr. Alexi asked, "Leon, when can you start?"

I said, "I should give a week's notice."

Mr. Alexi walked me around the floor. He introduced me to Nick Gold and Paul Mason. They were young guys, my age. Nick lived in Arlington and Paul lived on the North Shore. By then, it was six o'clock but they weren't going home. They put in as many hours as they wanted.

Plenty of work. I knew my friends at Forbes Lithograph would be happy for me. Forbes was a dump compared to this Tracer Labs.

Gee, I'd be working in the city. I could walk to Washington Street. Filene's Basement. The jeweler where Aunt Alice and I bought Estelle's ring. And the pay was much better. I was going from sixty-one dollars a week to one hundred-two dollars a week. We went back to Mr. Alexi's office and he shook my hand. He said, "Welcome to Tracer Labs." I couldn't wait to get home and tell Estelle. A draftsman. Double the salary. I was moving up. Nothing could stop me now.

Leon Rubinstein and his wife Estelle, Natick, Massachusetts, 1958.

The End

Looking Back: A Conversation with Leon Rubinstein

Why is it important for you to write a memoir?

Well, I'm seventy-eight years old. Never thought I'd get to this age. But here I am. Lots of free time on my hands. Life becomes very lonely in this stage of life. There isn't a day that goes by, or a week, where I don't lose a friend. In the past, I didn't reach out. Somehow stayed away because the stories we shared were on the sad end of things, and life would be not improving because of these stories. I wanted to stay away from negative thinking. Because my outlook on my life is always positive. Now there are so few of us left. So, I've decided to leave something behind.

I want my children to wake up and talk about it. That I survived the Holocaust. There will be a point in their lives when they get to be my age. When they have more time on their hands. I have a feeling they'll want to know more. What happened in my life time. They'll be glad I told my story. Hopefully, through my experiences they will be in contact with people. And maybe convince them to look in a positive direction. Terrible things took place in my lifetime and God knows they are still taking place in the world today. They will take place tomorrow.

Estelle and Leon Rubinstein, Concord, Massachusetts, 1992.

And they'll take place after I'm gone. Maybe my grandchildren or grandchildren's children will convince somebody that these things shouldn't take place. This is the reason I decided to talk about what happened.

I think it's a pretty good reason. There are a lot of Rubinsteins out there. Maybe one of my descendants can contribute something that will change the attitude of people so they won't behave the way they do. I don't know why people abuse one another. Why they instigate. Why they go out and commit such atrocities. It's beyond my belief. Hopefully, my story will help in the future.

What person influenced you the most in your life?

That will bring some tears to my eyes. It was my father, the man in the house. Everybody depended on him. Looked up to him. He was the timekeeper, the coach, the teacher. He was all. The one that made the rules to live by. And we didn't question those rules. He knew children learned more by example than any other way.

You couldn't help but admire my father. There was nothing he couldn't do. He could prepare food for almost an army. And there would be no mess. Sometimes now I observe a friend cooking a fancy dish with all sorts of recipes and measuring cups and spices. Back then, I don't think my father had a measuring cup. But he knew the exact amount. If my father came to this country, he'd be the greatest baker. The greatest cook. The greatest achiever.

When I was growing up, he was always around. Day and night. In the morning when he left for work, I saw him. On the way back from school, I stopped by his workshop. After my chores and studies, he was there. He didn't connect by phone, but he sure connected with me. And I obeyed him. He was the most influential person in my life. Nobody could take his place. He was my dad, until today.

After surviving the Holocaust, how did you become such a confident person?

I was fortunate to survive the Holocaust. By listening to what my daddy would have done in each situation, I eventually found myself in Israel at age 16. I could focus on all the difficulties I had. As a child, as a teenager, as a young man. So many incidents come to mind. In spite of all of it, though, I was such a secure individual. So sure about myself. I knew where I was going and what my goals were. Maybe because of everything I went through. The hardships. The hunger. Somebody else would be marked by this and wouldn't be able to go on. I was marked but it didn't stop me. I think it helped that I had youth and health. And my looks didn't hurt. I knew that as long as I was healthy, I could always earn for myself. And I didn't need much. For long stretches of my early life, I had only myself to rely on. Maybe that's why I believed in myself.

Did you have a moment in your life that felt like a turning point?

My turning point was when I connected with relatives in America. It was so difficult to do. Families were secretive in those days. A house was like a beehive. It was enclosed. Everything that took place in the house stayed there. There was very little that I knew as a child about my relatives outside of Poland. There was one name that appeared and stuck in my mind. The family name of Weiner, which was my mother's side of the family. I didn't know how it was spelled. But I just so happened to spell it the right way. For some reason, my landsmen in Haifa realized that the Weiner family in Boston was related to this boy in Israel. People were skeptical in this country that a stranger wanted to connect with the Weiners. It wasn't just any family. They were well-to-do, business people. Connecting with those relatives was a pivotal moment. And I made it happen. It was my perseverance. My drive. My chutzpah. It was a hard, hard fought battle to get to America. And once I came here, there was no way of stopping me. I came to the land of plenty. I was never hungry, never thirsty. Never out of anything. I had my hands and I knew how to work.

I'm so grateful for finding my way to America. This is my country. Sure, we're not always doing the right thing. But I vote. I participate. I contribute. I'm part of it.

When you were a child, how did you view the roles of men and women?
You have to picture the childhood I had. The adults I came in contact with while I was at school. My teachers. The adults I saw when I took a hair cut. When I bought a pair of shoes, which didn't happen too often. Grown-ups meant everything. Especially the male. He was the dominant force. He controlled everything. It's a different world we live in today. Those days, the male was God. Wouldn't dare stand up to him. The males in my immediate family were my dad, my grandfather and my uncles. They were gods. The women, as hard as they worked, they didn't bring in an income. For some reason, they were just doing chores.

My mother and father were on the same page because of the needs of the family. But my mother was submissive. She would listen. I never heard my mother voice her opinion about anything. It might have happened behind closed doors. My mother did a lot. No doubt about it. Taking care of the children, maintaining the home, preparing the meals. But she was overshadowed. I saw my father as being the man that made things happen. My mother never complained about anything. Even when the war broke out and there was panic and we knew what was going on in the world to a certain extent. Even then my mother never expressed her ideas about what to do for the family. She deferred to my father. And God knows how hard he tried. That was how things were back then. For the most part, the men made the decisions and the women went along.

As a child, what was it like to grow up with six siblings?

I've got to tell you something I observed in the animal kingdom. I was visiting my daughter last Thanksgiving and I was exposed to her dogs. She has a German Shepherd, maybe three years old. And she took in a young Siberian Husky. The puppy was about a year and a half, almost the same size as the adult dog. But the German Shepherd was in charge. If that puppy didn't listen to my daughter's commands, the German Shepherd was ready to kill him. If the puppy didn't behave.

It brought back my childhood. Because my siblings would have killed me if I was to rebel. That observation of the dogs triggered my memories of what took place. Not only my family. Every family. My cousin's family. It was a chain of command. The big ones took care of the little ones. The little ones were depending on them. Not depending so much on the mother and father. Depending on the sister to help you get dressed. To help put your shoes on, which didn't fit because they were a hand-me-down. To help with the sleeves that were three times longer than they should have been. Nobody shortened them because they'll belong to another child that's going to come. Sure, the shirt you're wearing now is your brother's shirt. Somebody is going to wear it after you. Your brother's shirt is going to last until it falls apart. Same thing with a pair of slacks.

I never remember needing something I didn't get from a sibling. No matter how young they were or how old they were. They always reached out and gave a hand.

You and your only surviving sibling have different recollections of your childhoods.

After Ana fled the ghetto in 1942, I didn't see her again for twenty years. In 1962, Ana was living in Poland. She wrote a letter to a friend in Israel, who connected her to the Koretzor Society. That's how they tracked me down in America. Ana has her own story to tell. She wrote a book in Hebrew, *Ana Podgajecki: A Woman On The Run.* It was published by Yad Vashem in 2002. She showed it to me in 1996, when I was in Israel. Close to 700 pages. I wanted to read it. But she pulled it away because it wasn't to be read yet. I told her, "Once it's written, it's for people to read."

Yes, Ana and I have different accounts of growing up. According to my sister's calculations, I was born in 1937 and got married when I was thirteen years old. I have a description she wrote of what happened to our family. In the first paragraph it says, "Leon Rubinstein was born at the beginning of 1937. This is what my mother told me in 1942 at the time that they led her to her death." According to my calculations,

Ana wasn't even home at that time. She had already escaped the ghetto. When I bring it to her attention she says, "I don't remember a thing." But I think she remembers it all.

I speak to her once a month or every two weeks. The other day, she reminded me on the phone that I don't know everything because we were a family of eight children, not seven. Even though there is no name for the last child. But she claims there was another son. She was the only one that saw him. Now, I was with my mother a few days before she died. And I didn't see that child. She had my youngest sister Luba in her arms. It's so painful for me. My sister really believes in this eighth child. I can't verify who else saw him because there are only two of us alive. And we have different memories.

In those days, childbirth was not so easy. God knows there were often complications. In my family, it just so happened that no babies died at birth. But if you talk to Ana, there were some deaths. How many were they? She doesn't want to talk about it.

I wish I had a better life with my one remaining sister. But it's not my fault. My sister was traumatized because of what took place. We all were. Certain stories she remembers, I don't know where they came from. But those are the way she saw things. In my mind, I have a layout of my house on Manasterskya Street. In Ana's version, we lived in a castle. But the house I grew up in would fit in one corner of my home in Falmouth. With dirt floors. With windows that were mostly covered because there was glass to be replaced and it wasn't replaced. My sister saw things in life

Leon's sister, Ana Podgajecki with Leon, PetaTikva, Israel, 1996.

185

I never saw. Dreams about things that I never dreamed. But people see these things. Not only my sister. I've read stories that my contemporaries have written about their lives. They've seen things that I've never seen. And I've been in their houses. I know most of their families. They smelled flowers that I never smelled. They saw castles and I saw dumps. Maybe I look at them as dumps. Maybe they were castles.

What is Koretz like now?

I visited Koretz in 1994 and nothing has changed. If you walk into those homes today they look worse than when I left in 1945. Since 1945 they have not seen a coat of paint, these homes. Their roofs have collapsed, windows are broken. The floors are dirty. Still have outhouses. Still fetch their water from the Korchyk River for the needs of the family. For washing. Or cooking a pot of soup. Today the water is green because of pollution. That river, where the water used to be pristine. For some people, that was gold.

During that visit, I went to the area where my house once stood, before it was burned down. I was speaking with a woman that lived next door. The same woman that took over the house from a Jewish family in 1945. She wouldn't let me in the house in fear I would put claim to it. I had to remind her in her own language that my car was parked in a nicer place than she slept in. Don't worry about it. I didn't come to take anything. The bottom line is that's her home now. Her castle.

Aside from your sister Ana and the Weiner family, have you maintained contact with any other relatives?

In the 1980s, I connected with my father's sisters, Esther and Batsia. They were in their late seventies, living in Argentina. I found them in Buenos Aires through the help of the Koretzor Society. I wrote to them, explained who I was and immediately they invited Estelle and I to visit. We gathered at Esther's daughter's luxurious apartment. Communicated the best we could, since they spoke Spanish and just a bit of Yiddish.

While the meal was being prepared, Batsia brought me to a bedroom to speak privately. We sat on the bed and she turned to me. She was a heavyset woman, dressed plainly. Out of nowhere, in an operatic voice, she began singing the story of her life. It began, "My name is Batsia," and she sang about her hardships and struggles. Coming to Argentina, divorcing her first husband, working as a seamstress, marrying her second husband, raising her son. She grabbed my hand and put it on her breast so I could feel her heart beat. In a higher pitch, she sang about her son's marriage to a Catholic girl. How it pained her to see crucifixes hanging on the wall, her grandchildren attending church. Watching her son abandon the Jewish faith. For forty-five minutes she sang through her tears. It was difficult for me to treat her son sympathetically after that. After all she'd been through, how could he cause his mother such pain? This cousin of mine died recently but his children still keep in touch. They send me pictures of their families.

I have a few cousins who survived the war in Eastern Europe. The children of my mother's brothers and sisters. A couple of them made it to Israel. But I never maintained contact. Some of it was a language barrier, some of it was intermarriage problems. I didn't take lightly to that.

Here's a story. In 1994, I participated in a ceremony to honor the Jews of Koretz killed in the Holocaust. A fence and memorial stone were put up to mark the location of the mass graves. Here I was in a place where I'm not liked. Anybody that looked at me thought, how the hell did this guy survive? All the other Jews are buried. At the gravesite, a gentleman approached me with a young lady. In English, she asked if I came from the United States. And I said to her, "Yes." From her tone, I could tell these people weren't at the gravesite to commemorate the Jews. They were there to network.

The gentleman told his daughter to ask me, "Do I know anybody by the name of Beiner in the United States?" Well, in Russian or Ukrainian, the W is a B. So the word Beiner was actually Weiner. I put two and two together. This guy had to be a cousin of mine. He and his daughter asked more questions and I kept answering. After ten or so minutes, I asked the daughter to tell the father that I know him. We're cousins. He's the son of one of my uncles on my mother's side.

This cousin of mine told me his father passed away. He took out pictures of a Christian burial. After the father's first wife died, he remarried a Christian woman who buried him in her tradition. The family was no longer Jewish. Over one or two generations, they became completely Christian.

They invited me over to the house, about fifteen miles away in a nearby city. I told them I'd visit that night. He wanted to pick me up at the hotel, but I said, "No, thank you." Even though I was going to visit a cousin, I brought a bodyguard to accompany me. A good-sized guy, a policeman. Over there you don't go anyplace by yourself. You never know, those people might kill you for your scarf or your pen.

We drove to their apartment in a five-story building. The hallway was dark. Someone probably stole the bulb for his apartment. The bodyguard went there without a flashlight. He used matches. We walked up to the fourth floor. The atmosphere in the apartment was not that cordial. They set a table. Sliced up some salami. Slices of bread. A few apples. Everything was polluted. That area was hit hard by the Chernobyl explosion. The fruit was rotten. I didn't eat anything.

The bottom line was they wanted out of there. Looking for a ticket to America. Well, I don't consider Christians to be family. They turned their backs on their Jewish roots. So my connection wasn't that warm. I asked them, why don't you go to Israel? They didn't want to go because of the conflict between the Arabs and the Jews. They wanted to come to the United States. Well, needless to say, I wasn't really involved. They wanted me to get in touch with the rest of the family, with cousins. Which I did. I did my part. But I left it as such.

When I look back on it, I see how our relations were hurt because of the war. Because of the change that took place in people's lives. It's like a disease that never leaves. It's affected everything in life.

Was the family that hid you in the Ukraine different from other gentiles?
There's one thing about that family that saved me. There was no drinking going on. Because drinking is a way of life in that part of the world. I'm talking about hard liquor drinking. But that family, I don't remember anybody ever taking a drink. I can just picture this school friend of mine who was running the family. If he had taken out a bottle when his buddies got together on a Sunday, then I would have been the end of the party. They would have dragged me out and celebrated. The killing of Lazer Rubinstein. But I was fortunate. No drinking at all. My friend and his buddies created their own entertainment. Shooting off guns, horsing around. I always feared one of them would get wind that I was hiding. And for them, that would be a game. In the end, I was surprised they didn't turn against me. Hard to believe I wasn't pulled out and killed.

I looked up my friend's family during my visit to the Ukraine in 1994. And I found one of the daughters. She was my age, maybe a little older. Lived within a half a mile of the area with her husband. I went to her house but she didn't want to acknowledge she knew me. Even though I told her who I was and that I knew her as a young girl. Her husband walked right out. Didn't want any part of it. I looked around and pointed to family pictures but she shied away. Wouldn't admit that she knew me. Maybe because of fear of neighbors. Retribution. Who knows what memories she carries with her?

When the Russians found you in the potato field in May 1944, you were still in hiding even though the area had been liberated months before. Why do you think your friend's family didn't notify you of the Russian liberation?

Maybe they were holding me for a price. Maybe to exchange me for something. My friend was involved in anti-government activities. Maybe they were using me for something they could trade in case they would have to. I don't see any other reason why they wouldn't come get me and tell me I could go to the city. They could have chased me out at night. I don't know what was going on in their mind. There has to be a reason. Maybe fear? Maybe they thought I knew more than I knew. Maybe they were afraid I would turn the son in. But I wasn't aware of the type of activities the son was involved in. There was a reason they kept me. But I have no answer. And I'll never know why.

After the Russian liberation, what were relations like between Christians and Jews?

Keep in mind it was the local Christians who hunted us down like animals. They were our neighbors, our friends. Yet they had such hatred for us. After the Russian liberation, the Christians were still killing the Jews. Some of those people would put Jews in a room and set the room on fire. I knew of a Jewish man who survived the war just to be killed by a Christian family. Believe me, there was a lot of hostility toward the Christian community from the Jews. I'm talking the Jews wanted to kill the Christians that were killing the Jews. Even today, the wounds haven't healed. Anti-Semitism still exists in Poland. Absolutely. And it will for many, many years. No matter how much we educate. The hatred is there. And it flares up. It's easy to find a scapegoat. Blame it on the Jew.

What effect did the war have on you?

The war had a tremendous effect on me. In a way, the war made me who I am. I had to learn how to survive. How to find food. How to find people I could trust. There were many, many situations where I could have gone astray. But I stayed the course. I learned that from my dad. He had a phrase. "You can learn from everybody. Keep your eyes open." Even a drunk. Observe him. You can learn not to be one. A sick person, watch him. One that is homeless, watch. Because you can learn something. I benefited from that phrase. Especially when I was on my own during the war.

After I survived the Holocaust, I found myself in the War of Independence in Israel. Killing was happening every day. It wasn't publicized because we didn't have television. Newspapers were limited, too. Maybe once a month I would see a headline and pick it up. Radio was available. We knew what was going on. Did those wars make me a better person? I don't think so. I wish I wasn't exposed to that kind of violence. There's nothing like seeing flesh all over the place for no reason. Nobody wants to see that. It's one thing to read about. See it in pictures. The other thing is to be part of it.

These days, violence and I don't get along. I turn away from reading stories about violence. Never watch violent movies. I can't take it. And I hate wars because of my experiences. Never could I remember that a war accomplished anything. I can't understand it. Even this war we're fighting in Iraq. People are killing neighbors. By hundreds, by thousands. Over nothing at all. I look at the kids that are dying. Nineteen and twenty year-old kids. Give them a chance to live. Those kids are there by circumstance. They enlisted because the government said they'd pay their education. Many of them come from broken homes. Nobody told them what war is all about. War changes the way you see the world. Changes the way you behave, the way you live your life. War destroys families. It breaks people down.

Is there a reason you waited until your seventies to tell your story?
The Holocaust was a topic never to be discussed. Never talked about it with my kids. I have friends that call me almost on a daily basis and we've never discussed the Holocaust. They don't know what happened to me. What they know is that I'm a good guy. A guy to share a joke with. A guy that made it. My own cousins, Sonny, Allen and Judy, know very little about me. And they're like brothers and sisters. When their parents wanted to know about the Holocaust, it was always in relation to their family. Even my wife doesn't know everything I went through. Not because it's a secret. But you can't discuss it with just anybody. Has to be discussed with people who lived through it. People who understand. When regular people learn I'm a survivor, they say, "You must have had quite a life." And that's where the conversation stops.

The last time I was in Israel was 1996. A group of us from Yagur went to visit Mashabei Sadeh. About twenty people gathered around. Husbands and wives and their children. They asked me to tell my story. But it wasn't easy. It took a while for me to start talking. A lot of coaching went on. Finally, I spoke up. There were tears. Believe me, not a dry eye. It was recorded on a tape and mailed to me. When I received it, I thought to myself, "That wasn't so bad, talking about what happened." In a way, that was preparation for this book.

Did you sustain your relationship with your Uncle Harry over the years?
My Uncle Harry was very tough on me, but I don't hold a grudge against him. In fact, later in life when he was alone and needed somebody to be with, I went to him. I left my wife and children to be there. So he wouldn't spend a night by himself. I have the best

relationship with his kids, because they saw what I did for him. We kiss each other on the lips when we get together. I'm close with the whole family, invited to every event. The Weiners are wonderful people. Sonny inherited the family business. Allen is a dentist, and Judy has a store of Judaica. Sadly, Ruth died of cancer, the same illness that took Aunt Alice. No doubt about it, Uncle Harry had quite a family.

Of what moment are you most proud?

My proudest moment was when my children were born. Debra and Wade. First my daughter came. I was in communication with the doctor that did the delivery. Dr. Jacob Mezer. He called me to say I have a little girl. In those days, we didn't know in advance if a boy or girl was coming. It was okay with me. I wouldn't have it any other way.

I rushed to Beth Israel Hospital in Brookline and got to see my little girl. She was born an hour before. With a nose still flattened out from being in the womb. Beautiful eyes. Beautiful hair. I was in tears. The same thing happened a few years later when my son was born. There I had one of each. Healthy babies. The doctor examined them, checked them over. They were perfect. Until today, I cry when I talk about my kids. Knock on wood. They're amazing.

Can you tell us about your decision to have children?

It was a tough decision. A private decision. You know, Estelle and I had a short courtship. I saw my bride sometimes twice a day, because we were in the same area in the city. And God knows, every time I saw her, I won her over. I was a charmer. Made her laugh. We talked about a lot of things, but we never discussed having children.

When we had enough money to buy a house, that's when we started talking about having a baby. At that time, I was commuting to work. I used to observe accidents. A lot of things went through my mind. I thought, "God forbid, what if something happened to me?" And I asked myself, "Do I really want children?" I started thinking about my own childhood. Sure, before the war, I had an incredible family. But once I lost my family, I lost my childhood. All this went through my mind. And when we were trying to conceive, it didn't click. When you have things on your mind, the rest of the body somehow knows.

At one point we talked about adopting. It was out of the question as far as I was concerned, because nobody wanted to adopt me when I was a kid. Nobody wanted any part of me. And I was such a good kid. As much as I tried to attach myself, attach myself to some family, it never happened. Maybe somebody threw a bone to me. A hunk of bread. But no one ever wanted to take me in and give me a family.

Another thing. When I was a young man of nineteen, I would visit Israeli families who knew me or knew part of my family, and I was an undesirable person in their eyes. If they had a daughter, God forbid she should get herself attached to me. Keep in mind I was a good-looking guy in those days. But some families, I wasn't welcome because they didn't want me around their daughters. It hurt. Being a person no one wanted. A person without a family. And the same thing happened when I first came to this country. I was a hunk. I spoke English. I knew how to behave. But certain families didn't want any part of me.

One girl I met at a dance. She gave me her telephone number to call. The next day, the girl's father got on the phone and warned me, "Stay away from my daughter." Even my good friend Jack Herschman didn't want me for a brother-in-law. The fact was he didn't know my past. He knew the identity I presented to him. But he didn't know my life before America. A lot of people wondered what really transpired between point A to point B. It was like I was in jail. I had to have been someplace. How else could I have survived? I was like a pariah. Born in the wrong place at the wrong time.

It took Estelle close to a year before she conceived. There were economics, too. We wanted to have a home before we brought in children. Five years after we married, I had a home that was partially paid for. A door to walk into with hinges that were paid for, with a lock that was paid for. And then I took that step. To become a father. Have a family of my own.

What is the importance of family in your life?
Family in my life is everything because family was everything when I was a child. And I can't help but extend that. I did everything in my power to make sure my family stayed together. We celebrated every occasion we could, as far as the children went. From year one, we celebrated birthdays. We had a tradition of buying the same special birthday cake at the bakery. We went to all of the functions at school. The musical performances, the baseball games. Every Friday night we celebrated Shabbat. That happened no matter what. We said Kiddush and lit Sabbath candles. And I always belonged to a temple. I made it my business to bring the children to temple so they could experience the traditions. There's a certain feeling when one goes to temple. You can't help but become part of it. When you're exposed week in and week out. Whenever the Weiners had a family event, I brought my children. Never went by myself. It was important for them to see that this was my family.

All that I know about family, I learned from my father. What I saw growing up was instilled in me. And I carried it on. It served me well. I know it served my wife well. She has a wonderful relationship with my daughter and son. Believe me, I don't take my family for granted.

Despite the differences in your upbringings, it sounds like you and Estelle have had a successful marriage.

Estelle has been an unbelievable mother and wife. And a great friend, too. She's terrific. She's also very good at taking care of herself. Appearance to her is important. Friends are important. And God knows, she's got a lot of them. She could have had a lot more if there was more backing from the family. I'm talking about the years before I came into her life. She was one of two children. Her older sister, Edith, was sick with childhood diabetes. In those days, they took it seriously. Estelle was deprived of sweets at home. She had second class citizenship, you might call it. The older one came first. So Edith had a nice wedding to Harold. When it came to Estelle getting married, there wasn't much money for that. It was the family that gave to one and not the other.

Her parents were very good people. They did the best they could with the experience and education they had. But it could have been better. Estelle was an A student. A member of the National Honor Society. For some reason, as Jewish families go, the push wasn't there. But all in all, with the tools she had, she did very well. This girl achieved a lot.

In 2002, after so many years of marriage, Estelle and I made a big celebration. Our first marriage was hardly anything. We decided to renew our vows and throw ourselves a party. We hired a kosher caterer to accommodate friends and family. The *simcha* was at our house in Falmouth. Cantor Scherr from Temple Israel officiated. My grandchildren held up the *chuppah*. We splurged on a beautiful *ketubah* that hangs in our living room. It was a wonderful, memorable day.

How do you think being a survivor affected your wife?

I think it affected Estelle much more than I realized. She knows a great deal about the Holocaust. She's read a lot. Even took courses on the Holocaust. But she's shied away from being close to other Holocaust survivors. Because they come with a certain amount of baggage. Sometimes discussions take place that aren't suited to her way of thinking.

Estelle tried to maintain a home that was one step above the type of people she grew up with. Not to speak with an accent. She wanted to move away from that. But being a Holocaust survivor, sometimes I'd get together with other survivors. A lot of my friends came to visit from Israel. These were my brothers and sisters from Yagur. Most of them had trouble speaking English, so we spoke Hebrew. That became a problem because my wife didn't want to be left out of the conversation. It became a problem again when we went to Israel in 1996. I was surrounded by friends and she felt excluded.

Way back when the children were little, Estelle and I discussed will they have an opportunity to learn another language. Be it Yiddish, Polish, Russian. I spoke all these languages fluently. Nope. Estelle didn't want me to speak to the kids in a foreign language. And today, they wish I did speak to them in Yiddish. Especially my son. But Yiddish was not something that Estelle wanted to hear in the house. The issue was that since I lived in America, I ought to adjust to life in America and speak English. Everything else should be left outside. And I accommodated. I wanted to become Americanized. I never fought about these things.

I more or less tried to not talk about the Holocaust. Not to say anything negative that took place. Not to reminisce. All of the baggage I came with was pushed aside. But I couldn't isolate myself from it. The fact is that I am a survivor. I can't forget what happened. Eventually, things come out in the open. Sometimes I'd be with the family at a gathering. And there'd be a discussion about the Holocaust and what took place. My cousins would start asking questions because of family connections. One way or another, my past came up. Being a survivor is who I am. Whether you like it or not. It's a part of me that never goes away.

Do you think being a survivor affected your children?

I believe it did have an effect on my children. During Passover, I liked to introduce some literature. After all, the holiday is about celebrating freedom from oppression. So I would bring out a reading. Be it a poem. Be it an article that was interesting. Something that I read during the year or last month or two. A reading that was apropos to what was taking place in the news. I had a habit of wanting to read it aloud. I was called on this many times by my children. That the only reason I was presenting the reading was because of my background. Did it stop? It dwindled. It didn't really stop because I felt strongly about it.

Surely, being a survivor impacted my children, but I never discussed it with them. I know it affected Wade. He's interested in knowing what happened during the Holocaust. He knows my story better than anybody because he recorded it. As far as Debra, I think there's some negative feelings about it. Maybe she feels she could have had a better relationship with her dad if it wasn't for him being a survivor. I don't know if she would express it that way. I can't speak for her. So I really don't know.

My daughter. My son. Different people have different feelings. I raised them the best I could. I raised them with love. That's all I can say.

How do you think being a survivor affected your grandchildren?

I don't think I ever mentioned to my grandchildren that I survived the Holocaust. I had a discussion with my grandson Max the other day. I told him how precious he was. How special he was. And I told him there are only two men in this world that carry my name. One of them is his dad and the other one is him. Told him how proud I was that he became a bar mitzvah boy last September. We had a long conversation on the phone. Not a word was mentioned that I was a survivor. In this relationship, it was just a granddaddy talking to a grandson. No, I never discussed the Holocaust with my grandchildren. I don't need to have that discussion face to face. I am their grandfather first, before being a survivor.

What are your thoughts about Judaism?

Judaism is more than a religion. It's a way of life. No matter where I go, where I turn, I always come back to the Jews. I consider myself lucky to be part of the Jewish tradition. Even though it cost me so much. Judaism cost me my family. My relatives. It cost me everything. But I'm proud of being Jewish. This faith promotes such good values. When I look at the type of things the Jewish people are doing, it's beautiful. Helping others less fortunate. Giving back to the earth. The passing on of life and tradition. Reminding us of where we came from. The richness of it all.

The Jewish immigrants that came to America in the 1900s didn't come just as laborers. They came as educated people. Most of them were bilingual. They strived for a quality life. They came here empty-handed and look at what they've done. Their accomplishments are incredible. Such an industrious group of people.

Here's a funny thing. I've been reading in the papers, people have been coming out of the woodwork in Poland. They know they were brought up as Christians but they're leaning toward Judaism. They're old people today and they want to be Jews. Imagine that.

Why is attending temple important to you?

I've always affiliated with a temple. It gives me a community, a place to participate in special occasions. When my father-in-law and mother-in-law passed away, the temple was a place of comfort. If it wasn't for belonging to the temple, I don't think Estelle would have found the support one really needs after a father or mother dies. It was the same experience when her sister, Edith, passed away. Our temple embraced us in our grief. Helped us move on. To me, it was a big thing.

Going to temple was always great when my kids were growing up because they understood they were part of a community. I have a feeling that because I brought my children to temple, my daughter Debra continued with the tradition. She realized how important that is. Her three girls all had bat mitzvahs, which takes a lot of work. I encouraged my son Wade to pursue a temple. He found his own community and is very involved in temple life.

Temple is important to me. I benefited and my children benefited. It shows them that they're part of something bigger than they can imagine. As long as I live, I want to experience that.

How do you feel about young people who are intermarrying?

Everyone is entitled to make their own decisions in life. I'm not too happy about young people leaving Judaism but I welcome those marrying into the tradition. And I have a feeling the young people that are marrying into Jewish families are enriching this religion of mine. The numbers prove it. I see them bringing people back. They want to be a part of it. So I think we're gaining. I don't see Judaism dying out. Never going to happen. The religion is thriving because there are so many ways to be Jewish. Secular, Humanist, Reform, Orthodox. All types of Jews. I know of people who converted to Judaism and are raising their children Jewish. In fact, I've attended bar and bat mitzvahs for these children. It's a beautiful thing. Who would have thought that would happen?

Have you thought about having a bar mitzvah later in life?

When I was twelve years old, I was in hiding. There was no bar mitzvah for me. It was gone. But Estelle had one in 1991. I was in business at the time. I told myself that making that buck was more important than having a bar mitzvah as an adult. Am I sorry? I don't know. I wanted to give as much as I could to my family. And because of that, we always had plenty. Never short of anything. My kids had the best clothes, the best food. Oh, we had an abundance of food. The freezer was always packed.

So you see, I provided for my family instead of preparing for a bar mitzvah. When I needed food, I didn't have it. And it became one of my insecurities. Until today, when I open up my freezer or refrigerator, I throw stuff away because it's been there for six or seven months. At one time, I had three refrigerators in the house. Two in the basement and one upstairs. Somebody finally told me, "Leon, do you really need those?" When I moved to Falmouth, I had two refrigerators sitting downstairs collecting dust. That's the way I am. Strange guy, huh?

What are your thoughts about religion in general?

It has its good things. It has its merits. I think organized religion is good for the soul and mind of individuals. I was reading that religious people are happier people. It's a known fact that religious people are more family-oriented. Every day there's a new religion being formed here or there. If somebody wants to start a new religion, they'll start one. It happened years ago and it's happening today. There's a reason for religion. Nobody came from heaven and made it happen. People crave community. Some hunger for spiritual belonging. For those reasons, we created religions.

How do you feel about our society becoming increasingly more violent?

Well, that's what happens between people. But given the number of people on this earth, I think we're doing pretty well. Sure, there's killing going on. But as a society, we're not killing each other as much as everyone thinks. It seems to be a lot. After all, it's publicized.

Most people don't realize just how many people there are in the world. You have to go to China to see how many. When I went there with Estelle, we walked into a market place. Close to 6,000 bicycles were stacked up. All black. Each one belonged to a separate person. I don't know how they recognized them. If you want to know how populated we are, you have to go to China. Or India.

When I came to this country in the '50s, there were about 230 million people. Today there are 300 million people. We're expanding. I'm quite sure, in another fifty years there will be another 100 million people. They'll find their place here. New York is expecting to expand by another one million people in the next fifteen or twenty years. They're going to plant trees, make it a green city. New York. I don't know how it's going to happen. A million people within the next few years. Overall, with that many people, I think we're doing great as a society.

After everything you endured during the war, do you consider yourself to be a lucky man?

Extremely lucky. Surviving the Holocaust. Making it to Israel, where I was wounded twice in the army. Coming to this country. Finding Estelle. People looked at us and said, "It's not going to work. Two people from two different worlds." Making my marriage successful. Raising two beautiful children. Landing the right jobs. It's all been hard work. But I persevered. Because I felt indestructible. Young people feel that way.

Last December, I was in a head-on collision. I don't know how I came out alive when I see the pictures of my vehicle. I don't believe anyone is watching over me. It's just luck. After my accident, I went to the hospital in Taunton. I thanked the doctors and nurses for helping me through. I don't take anything for granted. I've been very, very lucky.

Did you experience post-traumatic stress after the war?

I had a situation in the 1970s when I was working at Polaroid as a mechanical engineer. One day, my head wasn't clear. I was leaving a building while the custodian was cleaning the glass door. I walked right into it. I didn't break the glass but it knocked me out. I woke up in the nursing station.

The nurses said, "Do you know what happened?"

I said, "They shouldn't have cleaned the doors."

At the time, I was feeling some stress. I was bored at Polaroid and wanted to branch out on my own. But Estelle was insecure about me leaving a steady job with a steady paycheck. So there was this conflict between me and my wife. When I had my fainting episode, the doctor recommended I see a psychiatrist. I made an appointment with him in Brookline. Now, I'm not a smoker. And this psychiatrist was sitting behind his desk in his smoky little office. I went there once, maybe twice. I said to myself, "The person that really needs a psychiatrist is the doctor. Not me." And that was the end of it.

Therapy was something I never needed. I coped on my own. And thank God it worked for me. I don't think it's bad to talk to somebody. Even my rabbi, Rabbi Kushner, recommended that I talk to a professional. You know, the suicide rate among Holocaust survivors is high. Especially in later years. Rabbi Kushner told me about a man who became famous writing books about helping Holocaust survivors. He said, "Leon, a person like him you should be talking to." Well, I never went to see that famous guy. My way has been working for me. I find pleasure in talking to my friends who went through what I went through. After my car accident, they called me and said, "Leon, pull yourself together. You made it through worse things than this." Those were very good calls.

You've always had a strong work ethic.

When I see people, two or three years without work, how could that be? I hear people today saying, "I can't get a job. Doesn't meet my needs." Well, I always found jobs that met my needs. Even when I had a full time job and wanted to make more money, I'd get another job on my week vacation. I knew someday I could use that money. Sure, people have a profession. They want to be working within that profession. Or they say, "Hey, I wasn't going to work for less than that." My philosophy is not every job has to pay, but all the jobs will pay. I always believed I've got to work. And no work was beneath me.

People come to my house in Falmouth and there's a lot to be admired. I built it all with my own two hands. Nobody ever gave me a dime. I speak with pride. My kids know it's a big thing. They know how it came. By making an honest dollar through hard work.

Do you forgive the perpetrators of the Holocaust?

How can one forget the Holocaust? One can't forget. And if one can't forget, how can one forgive? No. I will never forgive. I don't know what made people do such terrible things. What bothers me more is listening to the grandchildren of the perpetrators. They haven't learned a thing. I want to ask them, "Do you know where you come from? Do you know what your granddaddy did? Do you ever inquire?" The bottom line, they think exactly the same as their grandparents thought.

When I was on the S.S. LaGuardia from Israel in 1951, I was sitting and talking to a German kid. My age, twenty-one years old. He was talking hate. How the Germans had the right idea to get rid of the Jews. This was an educated kid, coming to the United States as a student. A nice, good-looking German kid. Spoke a beautiful English. And it wasn't a one-time conversation. He sought me out to remind me that his grandchildren would do the same thing. Since then I had many, many similar conversations.

At Polaroid, I worked with a guy that was married to a German girl. She'd been one of the children volunteers in Hitler's army. He and I used to play tennis. After tennis, we'd go over his house in Millis. Have a beer and he'd make me a hamburger. We'd sit there and listen to his wife talk. She was my age, an intelligent German woman. And she was very proud of what she did. She'd say, "Look, it's a philosophy. It had to take place. It didn't succeed. But it will succeed some day." What was I supposed to do? Tear her eyes out? That conversation meant nothing to her. Needless to say, that friendship didn't go far.

Discussions take place like this every day. Go to a café in Germany and listen. My friend Diamond lives in Germany. A Holocaust survivor. He's exposed to these anti-Semitic conversations. The government provided him a nice pension because of the guilt they feel toward the few Jews that survived. He comes to Florida for the winter. Only sees doctors in the United States. Diamond won't go to a German doctor because he thinks they might kill him.

Have you made peace with your past?

No. I can't have peace because of my past. Those memories linger on. They never go away. Estelle can't sleep because of my dreams. I'm hardly sleeping. Just closing my eyes for five minutes and all of a sudden there's a dream. Walking with my father through potato fields, looking for hiding places. Talking to my commander in Rovno. Driving a military jeep. This is how I know I slept. Because I dreamed. Even today, I wake up yelling and fighting for my survival. I can never, never let go of what took place. It's like a broken record. Keeps on repeating itself. The same thing over and over again. There are a lot of people like me walking around with so much pain. Thank God I'm managing my pain. It's there every day. When I talk to my friends who survived the war, they have the same thing.

I can get away from my pain by getting involved in a book. If I can sit for a few hours and read, I know I wasn't thinking about anything else. Sometimes I go to the beach and watch the ocean. Sit on my favorite rocks, listen to music. This is the way I keep my mind occupied. In my house, I have a hobby shop for my projects and experiments. Again, it keeps me focused. So my mind doesn't wander.

The bottom line. I can never let go of what took place. That's why some people shorten their life because they don't want the pain to continue. I can understand that. It's not something I want to do, because I love my life. And I know many people who wish they were in my shoes. Believe me, sometimes they're very uncomfortable shoes but they wish they were there.

What would you like to say to your children and grandchildren about your life story?

It's hard for me to talk about one life story because I've had a lot of lives. Before Leon, I was Lazer, Vasili and Eliezer. So many stories. Many of them go untold. I hope my children and grandchildren learn something from a person like me. To see that no matter how tough life is, you can always make things happen, providing you put your mind to it.

I hope when they read my memoir and see all the obstacles in my way, they'll learn not to give up. Remember the way I approached things. I hope they learn something from that. And realize if they think a door is closed, it's not always closed. They just have to know how to open it. And if they think that road is blocked, it's not always blocked. They just have to go through it.

There are always obstacles. That's what life is all about. People get hurt. People get sick. People overcome these things. You have to move on. I know people that go on a holiday and find themselves stuck for three days in an airport. I've been in these situations. Turn around and go back and start over again. Sometimes you have a cloudy day. Wake up and make your own sunshine. I get up and make things happen every day. I'm an optimistic person. I like myself the way I am. If you don't like yourself, who is going to like you? I hope my grandchildren learn something from that. God knows, I've had a long stretch of life. There have been obstacles in my way for many, many years. Sure, there were rough days. But I made it through. Always thankful. Always glad. That's the type of person I am.

I hope my children and grandchildren appreciate they have something written down about my life. I can't pick up anything and read about my dad. I don't have any letters that he wrote. I've been looking for one for a long, long time. In Argentina, in Israel, in America. But I couldn't locate one. Though I made great efforts. I want my offspring to go to their bookshelf and say, "This is my granddaddy." They don't have to read the whole book. They can spend a little time reading one chapter. That's enough. Many people today can't read about their parents and grandparents because nothing was written. Or nothing was saved.

Is there a message you'd like to convey to other people who read your memoir?
Maybe, maybe what I lived through might change one mind. Someone might think that what happened to me shouldn't happen to a little boy. Children should have a more normal life. I'm hoping this book I'm leaving behind will convince one individual that what took place was terribly wrong. That itself would accomplish all. If one person could be changed.

So few of us survived the Holocaust. We're talking a few hundred thousand, out of a population of six million. If ten percent left something behind like a memoir, it could change some minds. A reader might think, "Look at these people. The way they suffered. Look at what they went through." That understanding would be everything.

What's your wish for the world?
I wish for the world to have better leaders to give us guidance. Our society needs to smarten up and realize we can't rape the earth like we're doing. When I travel the world today, I see how polluted it is. How it's being abused. If we're not going to take care of the earth, nobody else will. The average person doesn't realize what he's doing to this world. He should take public transportation instead of drive. Use less water. If society continues the way it is, we're going to be overpopulated. We've got to take care of things. We've got to stop fighting each other. So we

can leave this world a better place for our children and our children's children.

Considering everywhere you've lived and traveled, what is the most significant place for you?

This country is my home. No matter where I go, and God knows I've been many, many places, I come back here and feel like kissing the ground. Estelle and I have a beautiful home in Falmouth. It's so peaceful. I can go out on my back porch and lay there and nobody is bothering me. There are twenty-six families on my street. But I think I'm the only one. I take a walk, six or seven o'clock in the morning. I don't see any cars. Just the blue sky and the smell of the ocean. This place is heaven for me.

Leon's children and grandchildren, Concord, Massachusetts, 2007.
From left: Robyn Peak, Laurel Peak, Gary Peak, Sydney Peak, Debra Peak, Ellie Rubinstein, Wade Rubinstein, Max Rubinstein, Jill Block, Estelle Rubinstein and Leon Rubinstein

Epilogue

In the fifty-four years since my return to the United States, I've had many blessings: my family, my career and my interests. Estelle and I have been married for fifty-five years. We have two children, Debra and Wade. Between them, we have five wonderful grandchildren: Laurel, Robyn, Sydney, Max and Ellie. This is my family, my pride and joy. When you have a family, you have everything.

In 1957, I became an American citizen. For twenty-eight years, I was employed as a technical specialist and project engineer at Polaroid Corporation. I couldn't have had a better job. I contributed my mechanical talents to the development of new technologies and consumer products. I was rewarded with numerous patents. During the early 1980s I started my own company, Innovative Prototype. I provided product development services to multiple clients, including Milton Bradley, A.T. Cross, General Scanning, Design Continuum, Boston Scientific, Digital Equipment Corporation, Wang Laboratories, The Museum of Science, Rogers Corporation, Atari and Apple Computer.

I have always been athletic. I love racquet sports and have played league badminton, table tennis and tennis. I enjoy competition and have won many trophies. For many years I was also a daily runner. I ran the Ocean State Marathon twice with a personal best of three hours and forty-seven minutes. I set a good example for my children, who have both run marathons.

Over the years, I've owned my own home, as well as owned and managed commercial real estate. I am most proud of designing and building my current residence in Falmouth, Massachusetts.

When I arrived in the United States in 1954, I joined the Koretzor Society. I've served on the board as treasurer and president. In the early '90s, I raised money to place a marker on the mass graves in Kozak, outside of Koretz. In 1994, I was present in Koretz when the marker was dedicated. My return to Koretz was a painful reminder of my childhood and the loss of family, friends and neighbors. Though I returned after fifty years, physically the town had changed little, as though frozen in time. Spiritually, the town was dead to me. The Jews were gone.

Leon Rubinstein
April 2008

Glossary of Terms

Aliyah The honor of being called to recite blessings for the Torah.
Bar mitzvah The ceremony marking the passage of boyhood to manhood at age 13.
Bensch To recite the blessing over the candles.
Bimah The raised platform where the Torah is read in shul.
Blintzes Pancakes with fillings.
Berachah Blessing.
Bris Circumcision ceremony for boys.
Challah Traditional braided bread for Shabbat.
Cholent Stew made of beans and barley, served on Saturdays.
Chometz Traces of leavened bread, disposed of before Passover.
Chuppah Jewish wedding canopy.
Daven To pray.
Eretz Yisrael The Land of Israel.
Gefilte fish Chopped fish with seasonings, traditionally served cold.
Gorgle Cooked chicken neck.
Grivens Chicken skin sautéed until crispy.
Ha'apala The illegal immigration of Jewish refugees from Europe to British Palestine.
Haftarah Readings to conclude Torah services.
Haganah Jewish paramilitary in British Palestine.
Haggadah The book telling the story of Passover.
Haroset A mixture of fruit, wine and honey used during Passover seders.
Hazzan Cantor.
Irgun The militant splinter group of the Haganah, resisting the British in Palestine.
Kaddish The prayer to honor the dead.
Karpas A green vegetable used during Passover seders.
Ketubah Jewish wedding contract.
Kibbitz To chit-chat.
Kibbutz A collective Israeli farm.
Kibbutznik A pioneer on the kibbutz.
Kiddush Blessing over the wine on holidays.
Knaidlach Dumplings.
Knishes Little pies baked with fillings.
Kosher According to the laws of kashrut, foods that are fit for consumption.
Kreplach Pasta stuffed with fillings.
Lebania Plain yogurt.

Maccabee Jewish athletic organization.

Maror Bitter herbs used during Passover seders.

Matzo Unleavened baked crackers eaten during Passover.

Mishpachah Family.

Mogen David Six-pointed star of David.

Motzi Blessing over the challah.

Mushav A privately owned farm.

Palmach The elite striking force of Haganah.

Passover The holiday celebrating the Jewish exodus from Egypt.

Patchier Gelatinous dish made of bone marrow and garlic.

Purim The holiday celebrating the rescue of Jewish people from destruction.

Rosh Hashanah The Jewish New Year.

Sabra Native-born Israeli.

Schlep To lug or carry with effort.

Schmaltz Chicken fat.

Seder Defined as "order" in Hebrew, it refers to the structured meal at Passover.

Shabbos/Shabbat Sabbath.

Shiddach An arranged marriage.

Shochet A kosher butcher.

Shofar A ram's horn, typically blown on Rosh Hashanah.

Shomer Shabbos A person who strictly observes the Jewish laws relevant to Shabbat.

Shul Synagogue.

Siddurim Prayer books.

Simcha A joyous event.

Simchas Torah The holiday marking the beginning and end of the annual Torah reading cycle.

Sukkot The holiday celebrating the fall harvest.

Tallis Prayer shawl.

Tanakh The Hebrew bible.

Tarbut Hebrew School in Poland.

Tefillin Leather boxes worn on the foreheads and arms of Torah-observant Jews.

Yasher Koach An expression of praise or thanks for serving in a religious role.

Yom Kippur Day of Atonement, the holiest day on the Jewish calendar.

About the Authors

Leon Rubinstein was born in the town of Koretz, Poland in 1930. Leon's life was cast into turmoil by the Second World War. Hidden on a farm, Leon miraculously survived the Holocaust. Following the war, he fled Eastern Europe for Palestine and eventually emigrated to the United States. He pursued a successful career as a mechanical engineer and small business owner. A tireless inventor, he has 35 patents in the fields of optics, plastics, and electronics. Father of two and grandfather of five, he lives with his wife in Falmouth, Massachusetts.

Emily Rubin's writing has appeared in anthologies, magazines and newspapers. She lives with her family in Concord, Massachusetts.

Printed in the United States
148072LV00001B/4/P

9 780911 051032